Abomination
of
Desolation

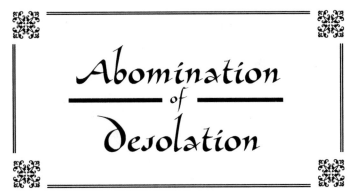

Abomination
of
Desolation

Ezekiel's and Daniel's Prophecies of the Last Days

Monte S. Nyman

CFI
Springville, Utah

ISBN 13: 978-1-55517-901-0
ISBN 10: 1-55517-901-0
v.2

Published by CFI, an imprint of Cedar Fort, Inc., 925 N. Main, Springville, UT, 84663
Distributed by Cedar Fort, Inc. www.cedarfort.com

Cover design by Nicole Williams
Cover design © 2006 by Lyle Mortimer
Printed in the United States of America

10 9 8 7 6 5 4 3 2 1

Printed on acid-free paper

Table of Contents

The historical Setting

To members of The Church of Jesus Christ of Latter-day Saints, Ezekiel and Daniel are well-known Old Testament prophets. Ezekiel is known for his prophecy of the two sticks, the Bible and the Book of Mormon, coming together as one in the last days. Daniel is known to all the Christian world for his great faith in keeping the Jewish health, or food laws, and for his miraculous deliverance from the lions' den. To Latter-day Saints, he is also known for his interpretation of King Nebuchadnezzar's dream regarding the stone cut out of the mountain without hands, which represents the restoration of the kingdom of God in these last days. However, other prophecies and principles given by these two ancient prophets are significant to Latter-day Saints. This book is an attempt to illuminate their teachings and prophecies.

The call of Ezekiel
(Ezekiel 1:1-3)

1. Now it came to pass in the thirtieth year, in the fourth month, in the fifth day of the month, as I was among the captives by the river of Chebar, that the heavens were opened, and I saw

visions of God.

2. In the fifth day of the month, which was the fifth year of king Jehoiachin's captivity,

3. The word of the lord came expressly unto Ezekiel the priest, the son of Buzi, in the land of the Chaldeans by the river Chebar; and the hand of the Lord was there upon him.

The book of Ezekiel begins "in the thirtieth year" (1:1), but does not specify in what time period. There have been many suggestions for the time period of the thirtieth year; the most prevalent seems to be Ezekiel's own age. Four years after the captivity and exile of Jehoiachin, Ezekiel's wife died (Ezekiel 24:15–18). Therefore, he was old enough to have married. The call of Ezekiel to prophesy was five years after Judah was taken into exile by Babylon, or the fifth year of Jehoiachin's captivity (Ezekiel 1:2–3). Consequently, he would have been twenty-five when he left Jerusalem if he were called in his thirtieth year. Twenty-five could certainly have been considered young.

The accepted date when the Jews were taken into captivity by Babylon varies among scholars. This text will use the dates given in the Chronology Chart of the Latter-day Saint edition of the King James Version of the Bible and will call the dates "traditional dating." In about 609 B.C., Jehoahaz was anointed king of Judah. He only reigned three months and did evil in the sight of the Lord. He was captured by Pharaoh-nechoh and taken into Egypt, where he died. After Jehoahaz was captured, his brother Jehoiakim was appointed puppet king by the Pharaoh and reigned for eleven years. He also did evil in the sight of the Lord (2 Kings 23:31–37). Nebuchadnezzar, king of Babylon, came to Jerusalem and captured Jehoiakim (2 Kings 24:1; 2 Chronicles 36:1–6). According to the Book of Daniel, this captivity came in the third year of Jehoiakim's reign (607 B.C., traditional dating), and the Babylonians carried off many treasures of the temple as well as certain of the children of Israel. Daniel was among them (Daniel 1:1–7). This is often called "the first wave" of Judah being taken into captivity by Nebuchadnezzar.

Jehoiakim served Nebuchadnezzar in Jerusalem for three years before he rebelled (2 Kings 24:1). The records do not say how long this rebellion lasted; but, as warned by the prophets, after several attacks upon Judah (2 Kings 24:2–4), Jehoiakim was taken captive and his son Jehoiachin reigned in his stead (2 Chronicles 36:6–8).

After reigning only three months, Jehoiachin was taken captive to Babylon and with him "all the princes, and all the mighty men of valour, even ten thousand captives, and all the craftsmen and smiths: none remained, save the poorest sort of the people of the land" (2 Kings 24:14). Ezekiel was among these captives, who are referred to as "the second wave" of Judah being taken into captivity. The two waves of captives taken to Babylon illustrate the beginning of the principle taught in the Book of Mormon that the Lord "leadeth away the righteous into precious lands, and the wicked he destroyeth, and curseth the land unto them for their sakes" (1 Nephi 17:38).

However, in his mercy, the Lord always forewarns a people through his prophets before he destroys their nation or land (2 Nephi 25:9). The prophets who warned Judah did not go into captivity, but Daniel and Ezekiel were raised up as prophets among those thousands taken into captivity, Daniel among the "first wave," and Ezekiel among the "second wave."

The fifth article of faith of The Church of Jesus Christ of Latter-day Saints declares, "We believe that a man must be called of God, by prophecy, and by the laying on of hands by those who are in authority, to preach the Gospel and administer in the ordinances thereof." This declaration is consistent with biblical teachings. In the New Testament we read, "And no man taketh this honour unto himself, but he that is called of God, as was Aaron" (Hebrews 5:4). The Lord also chose his twelve Apostles by revelation; he spent all night in "prayer to God" before choosing them (Luke 6:12). He later taught them, "Ye have not chosen me, but I have chosen you, and ordained you" (John 15:16). The same governing principle called both Ezekiel and Daniel to be prophets.

The Book of Ezekiel divides into three natural sections. The first twenty-four chapters are prophecies concerning the fall and captivity of the nation of Judah to Babylon under King Nebuchadnezzar. Chapters 25 through 32 are prophecies about Judah's neighboring nations. The third division, chapters 33 through 48, are prophecies of the latter days. These latter chapters can also be divided into three sections. Chapters 33 through 37 are concerning the restoration of the whole house of Israel under one king, the latter-day prince of David. Chapters 38 and 39 prophesy of the battle of Gog and Magog in the last days. The last nine chapters, 40 through 48, describe the latter-day temple to be built in Jerusalem.

The first five chapters of Ezekiel seem to be a continuous revelation given while Ezekiel was camped on the river of Chebar (in Babylon) with others who had been taken captive in the second wave of prisoners (2 Kings 24:14–16). It seems evident that God designated Ezekiel to be the prophet through visions and the Lord's voice, but he undoubtedly received an earthly ordination as well.

Ezekiel is called "the priest, the son of Buzi" (Ezekiel 1:3). He was not only a Levite, but also held the Melchizedek priesthood. The Prophet Joseph Smith taught, "All the prophets had the Melchizedek priesthood and were ordained by God himself. In other words, God called and designated them, but they would have had an earthly ordination as well. The Lord had the Prophet and Oliver Cowdery ordain each other after they had been ordained by angelic beings (see Joseph Smith–History 1:68–74). Who were the holders of the priesthood in Ezekiel's day? President Joseph Fielding Smith declared:

> When the Lord took Moses out of Israel, he took the higher priesthood also and left Israel with the lesser priesthood which holds the keys to the temporal salvation of mankind—the temporal gospel—that which deals with repentance and baptism particularly, but does not have to do with the higher ordinances which have been revealed in the dispensation in which we live [see D&C 84:25–27].
>
> Therefore, in Israel, the common people, the people generally, did not exercise the functions of priesthood in its fullness, but were confined in their labors and ministrations very largely to the Aaronic Priesthood. The withdrawal of the higher priesthood was from the people as a body, but the Lord still left among them men holding the Melchizedek Priesthood, with power to officiate in all its ordinances, so far as he determined that these ordinances should be granted unto the people. Therefore Samuel, Isaiah, Jeremiah, Daniel, Ezekiel, Elijah, and others of the prophets held the Melchizedek Priesthood, and their prophesying and their instructions to the people were directed by the Spirit of the Lord and made potent by virtue of that priesthood which was not made manifest generally among the people of Israel during all these years.
>
> We may presume, with good reason, that never was there a time when there was not at least one man in Israel who held this

higher priesthood (receiving it by special dispensation) and who was authorized to officiate in the ordinances, but this power and authority was withdrawn from among the people and they were denied the privilege of the ordinances which pertain to the fullness of glory, or the entering into the rest of the Lord.[1]

Ezekiel was faithful in his priesthood duties and was named by the Prophet Joseph Smith as a recipient of the Second Comforter. As this study will show, Ezekiel certainly had the visions of heaven opened to him. His prophecies are cited in the Doctrine and Covenants as speaking of things "which have not come to pass, but surely must" (D&C 29:21). Consequently, Ezekiel's teachings hold significant meaning for Latter-day Saints.

Daniel is of no lesser stature than Ezekiel. The Lord cites Daniel in two different chapters of Ezekiel (14 and 28). The Savior referred to him as a prophet and to his prophecies as he instructed his disciples on the Mount of Olives during the last week of his earthly ministry (Joseph Smith–Matthew 1:12, 32). He is similarly cited in the Doctrine and Covenants (116:1). Many Bible scholars reject Daniel as the author of the book bearing his name; the reasons are many and will not be discussed specifically herein. However, there are many prophets and apostles during and after the Prophet's day who accepted Daniel and his writings. Many of them are quoted in this work, but there are many others too numerous to mention or quote throughout. Therefore, this work accepts Daniel as the author of the book attributed to him.

The Book of Daniel also has two distinct sections: the faith-promoting accounts of Daniel and Shadrach, Meshach, and Abednego found in the first six chapters, and the four visions of the future shown to and interpreted by Daniel (although the second chapter also gives Daniel's interpretation of King Nebuchadnezzar's dream). The first chapters contain some of the most well-known stories in the Bible. Some of the accounts are better known than others, but all are used worldwide in Christian Sunday schools.

The stories from these chapters in Daniel are paraphrased occasionally by general authorities to teach various lessons or principles of the gospel. The Prophet Joseph Smith made only one change in these chapters in his translation of the Bible, but he did use the principles taught in the stories in some of his sermons. There are also a few references in the Book of Mormon and Doctrine and Covenants that are

applicable to the text of Daniel. Because the story line is quite familiar to most readers, the complete text will not be quoted; only the
scriptures most pertinent to the comments will be given in this book.

Read carefully, these two books provide great insights for Latter-day
Saint readers. It is my hope that reading this book will encourage Latter-
day Saints to gain a greater appreciation for these prophets and for the
insights that can be gained from careful reading of the scriptures.

Note

1. Joseph Fielding Smith, *Doctrines of Salvation*, comp. Bruce R. McConkie,
   3 vols. (Salt Lake City: Bookcraft, 1954–56), 3:84–85; see also Joseph
   Fielding Smith, *Answers to Gospel Questions*, 5 vols. (Salt Lake City:
   Deseret Book, 1957–66), 4:180.

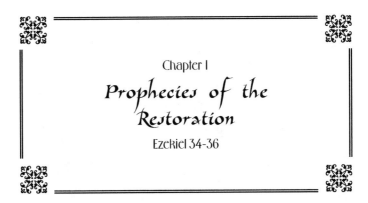

Chapter I

Prophecies of the Restoration

Ezekiel 34-36

esus taught the parable of the good shepherd to the wicked Pharisees (John 10:1–5). He identified himself as the good shepherd depicted in the parable as he explained the parable to them. The good shepherd knows each sheep by name, and the sheep know the shepherd's voice and respond to it. The shepherd loves his sheep and gives each one personal attention. He would lay down his life to protect his sheep. In the parable, the good shepherd is contrasted with the hireling shepherds, or the robbing and thieving Pharisees (John 10:6–18). If there are good shepherds, there are, by implication, poor shepherds. The words of Ezekiel, under consideration here, describe the wicked shepherds among the sheep of Israel in Ezekiel's day.

There are three revelations in chapters 34 through 36. The first revelation is "against the shepherds of Israel" (34:2), or the leadership of Israel. The time period extends from Ezekiel's day to the last days, or our own day. The second revelation is "against Mount Seir" (35:2) and is shorter than the other two. Mount Seir is in a range of mountains from the bottom of the Dead Sea through the land of Edom. Esau, Jacob's brother, and his descendants occupied the land of Edom in Bible times (see Genesis 36:8). Edom was also known as Idumea, which D&C 1:36 explains represents the world. This context of the chapter seems to be the Lord speaking to the world. The third revelation is given unto the mountains of Israel but not against them (Ezekiel 36:1). The content of the revelation strongly suggests that it is addressed to the Americas, which were given to the tribe of Joseph by the Father, through Jesus when he visited the Nephites (3 Nephi 15:12–13). Chapters 34 and 36 are clearly prophecies of the restoration of the gospel to the house of Israel in these latter days. An outline of the three chapters is given below.

1. Ezekiel 34:1–10. The shepherds of Israel feed themselves but do not feed the flock.
   a. They have not cared for the sick or sought for the lost but have ruled with force (34:3–4).
   b. The sheep were scattered because they had no shepherd (34:5–6).
   c. The Lord will hold the shepherds accountable, and they will cease to feed themselves instead of his sheep (34:7–10).
2. Ezekiel 34:11–31. The Lord will search out his sheep, deliver them out of all places, and bring them to their own land.
   a. They will be fed in the high mountains of Israel and care for the hurt and sick (34:14–16).
   b. The Lord will judge between good cattle and evil cattle (34:17–22).
   c. The Lord will set up one shepherd over them, his servant David (34:23–24).
   d. The Lord will make a covenant of peace with his sheep and bless them. They will know he is the Lord and they are his sheep (34:25–31).
3. Ezekiel 35:1–15. The Lord is against Mount Seir and will make her most desolate.
   a. The first reason is because of her perpetual hatred and shedding of the blood of the children of Israel when their iniquity had an end (35:5–9).
   b. A second reason is that she has said she will possess Israel and Judah, which are the Lord's (35:10).
   c. The Lord will make himself known among them when he has judged them, and they will know he is the Lord (35:11–13).

     d. When the whole earth rejoices, the Lord will make her and all Idumea desolate, and they will know he is the Lord (35:14–15).

4. Ezekiel 36:1–15. The mountains of Israel are a possession unto the residue of the nations, or the Gentiles.

     a. The heathen (Gentiles) will bear their shame (36:6–7).

     b. The branches of Israel will yield fruit, the cities will be inhabited and the waste places built, and both man and beast will multiply (36:8–12).

     c. The land will no more devour men and bereave nations (36:13–15).

5. Ezekiel 36:16–38. The house of Israel will be gathered from among the heathen and brought to its own land.

     a. When the people of Israel dwelt in their own land, they defiled it and profaned the name of the Lord, so he scattered them among the heathen (36:16–20).

     b. The Lord scattered them for his holy name's sake. He will sanctify his great name by gathering his people again (36:21–24).

     c. The Lord will sprinkle clean water upon them and give them a new heart and a new spirit. They will dwell in the land given to their fathers; they will be blessed but will remember their former evil ways (36:25–32).

     d. Israel will dwell in the cities and build the waste places to become like the Garden of Eden, and the heathen (Gentiles) will know that the Lord built the ruined places (36:33–36).

     e. Israel will be increased with men like a flock at Jerusalem in her solemn feasts (36:37–38).

Notes and Commentary

Although chapters 34 and 36 are not as well known as chapter 37, they have been quoted often by the General Authorities. The Prophet Joseph referred to them a few times and made two very insignificant changes in his translation. Also, cross references to other prophets like Isaiah and Jeremiah give us clearer interpretations of many verses.

A prophecy against the shepherds of Israel
(Ezekiel 34:1–3)

And the word of the Lord came unto me, saying, Son of man, prophesy against the shepherds of Israel, prophesy, and say unto them, Thus saith the Lord God unto the shepherds; Woe be to the shepherds of Israel that do feed themselves! should not the shepherds feed the flocks? Ye eat the fat, and ye clothe you with the wool, ye kill them that are fed: but ye feed not the flock.

The Prophet Joseph Smith applied these verses to himself to refute some claims that he was no longer a prophet: "The only principle upon which they judge me is by comparing my acts with the foolish traditions of their fathers and nonsensical teachings of hireling priests, whose object and aim were to keep the people in ignorance for the sake of filthy lucre; or as the prophet says, to feed themselves, not the flock."[1]

Scattered because there is no shepherd
(Ezekiel 34:4–6)

The diseased have ye not strengthened, neither have ye healed that which was sick, neither have ye bound up that which was broken, neither have ye brought again that which was driven away, neither have ye sought that which was lost; but with force and with cruelty have ye ruled them. And they were scattered, because there is no shepherd: and they became meat to all the beasts of the field, when they were scattered. My sheep wandered through all the mountains, and upon every high hill: yea, my flock was scattered upon all the face of the earth, and none did search or seek after them.

These verses telling why the house of Israel had been scattered also reflect the neglected role of the current leaders or shepherds. The good shepherd loved his sheep and tenderly cared for all of them, especially the sick or injured. A shepherd's robe had a large pouch or pocket to place the injured or those in need. He herded them with tender loving care, not "with force and with cruelty" (34:4). Verses 5–6 are similar to a verse in Zechariah (13:7), foretelling the scattering of Judah after the crucifixion of Christ and quoted by Jesus after the Last Supper: "I will smite the shepherd, and the sheep shall be scattered" (Mark 14:27).

The shepherds are accountable
(Ezekiel 34:7-10)

Therefore, ye shepherds, hear the word of the Lord; as I live, saith the Lord God, surely because my flock became a prey, and my flock became meat to every beast of the field, because there was no shepherd, neither did my shepherds search for my flock, but the shepherds fed themselves, and fed not my flock; therefore, O ye shepherds, hear the word of the Lord; thus saith the Lord God; Behold, I am against the shepherds; and I will require my flock at their hand, and cause them to cease from feeding the flock; neither shall the shepherds feed themselves any more; for I will deliver my flock from their mouth, that they may not be meat for them.

Judah has been without a true shepherd, and the Lord will hold the appointed shepherds accountable. The neglectful shepherds will no longer feed the Lord's sheep or themselves (34:10).

Sheep gathered to their own lands
(Ezekiel 34:11-16)

For thus saith the Lord God; Behold, I, even I, will both search my sheep, and seek them out. As a shepherd seeketh out his flock in the day that he is among his sheep that are scattered; so will I seek out my sheep, and will deliver them out of all places where they have been scattered in the cloudy and dark day.

And I will bring them out from the people, and gather them from the countries, and will bring them to their own land, and feed them upon the mountains of Israel by the rivers, and in all the inhabited places of the country.

I will feed them in a good pasture, and upon the high mountains of Israel shall their fold be: there shall they lie in a good fold, and in a fat pasture shall they feed upon the mountains of Israel. I will feed my flock, and I will cause them to lie down, saith the Lord God.

I will seek that which was lost, and bring again that which was driven away, and will bind up that which was broken, and will strengthen that which was sick: but I will destroy the fat and the strong; I will feed them with judgment.

The Lord promises to gather his sheep after they have been scattered (34:11–12). His sheep will gather into two folds: the land of Jerusalem and the land of America. The Father instructed Jesus when he visited the Nephites to give the Americas to the tribe of Joseph (3 Nephi 15:12–13). In this context, it seems that both gathering places, Jerusalem and America, are being described by the plural tense in the "mountains of Israel" (34:13–14). The description of a good shepherd is given in verses 12 through 16. Note that the Lord God, or Christ, is the shepherd, and compare it to John 10:1–15, where he contrasts his role to that of a thief or robber. The Prophet Joseph referred to Ezekiel 34:11–13 and four other Old Testament scriptures (Joel 2:32; Isaiah 26:20–21; Jeremiah 31:12; Psalm 1:5) with this comment: "These are testimonies that the Good Shepherd will put forth His own sheep, and lead them out from all nations where they have been scattered in a cloudy and dark day, to Zion, and to Jerusalem; besides many more testimonies which might be brought."[2] The Prophet's statement supports the concept of people gathering to both Jerusalem and America (Zion).

Judged between good and evil cattle
(Ezekiel 34:17–22)

> And as for you, O my flock, thus saith the Lord God; Behold, I judge between cattle and cattle, between the rams and the he goats. Seemeth it a small thing unto you to have eaten up the good pasture, but ye must tread down with your feet the residue of your pastures? and to have drunk of the deep waters, but ye must foul the residue with your feet? And as for my flock, they eat that which ye have trodden with your feet; and they drink that which ye have fouled with your feet. Therefore thus saith the Lord God unto them; Behold, I, even I, will judge between the fat cattle and between the lean cattle. Because ye have thrust with side and with shoulder, and pushed all the diseased with your horns, till ye have scattered them abroad; Therefore will I save my flock, and they shall no more be a prey; and I will judge between cattle and cattle.

The judgment of the Lord referred to by Ezekiel (34:17) is not a separation of the sheep from the goats when "shall be gathered all nations: and he shall separate them one from another, as a shepherd divideth his sheep from the goats" (Matthew 25:32). Nor is it a separation of the members of the Church from the world, but rather "between cattle and cattle" or "the rams and the he goats" (34:17). In other words, it is a cleansing of the Church, a separation of the good from the bad, the righteous from the wicked. The parable of the net given in Matthew 13:47–49 teaches the same concept: "Again, the kingdom of heaven is like unto a net, that was cast into the sea, and gathered of every kind: Which, when it was full, they drew to shore, and sat down, and gathered the good into vessels, but cast the bad away. So shall it be at the end of the world: the angels shall come forth, and sever the wicked from among the just."

The Prophet Joseph Smith gave the following interpretation of this parable: "For the work of this pattern, behold the seed of Joseph, spreading forth the Gospel net upon the face of the earth, gathering of every kind, that the good may be saved in vessels prepared for that purpose, and the angels will take care of the bad. So shall it be at the end of the world—the angels shall come forth and sever the wicked from among the just, and cast them into the furnace of fire, and there shall be wailing and gnashing of teeth."[3]

Another witness to the cleansing of the Church in the last days was given in modern revelation:

> Very, verily, I say unto you, darkness covereth the earth, and gross darkness the minds of the people, and all flesh has become corrupt before my face. Behold, vengeance cometh speedily upon the inhabitants of the earth, a day of wrath, a day of burning, a day of desolation, of weeping, of mourning, and of lamentation; and as a whirlwind it shall come upon all the face of the earth, saith the Lord. And upon my house shall it begin, and from my house shall it go forth, saith the Lord; first among those among you, saith the Lord, who have professed to know my name and have not known me, and have blasphemed against me in the midst of my house, saith the Lord. (D&C 112:23–26)

David will be their shepherd
(Ezekiel 34:23–24)

And I will set up one shepherd over them, and he shall feed them, even my servant David; he shall feed them, and he shall be their shepherd. And I the Lord will be their God, and my servant David a prince among them; I the Lord have spoken it.

The setting up of one shepherd over the sheep of Israel is further evidence of the gathering in this chapter referring to both Jerusalem and America. More will be said of David, the one shepherd to feed the flock of Israel, in chapter 37. Suffice it to say here that David refers to Christ: "Behold, the days come, saith the Lord, that I will raise unto David a righteous Branch, and a King shall reign and prosper, and shall execute judgment and justice in the earth. In his days Judah shall be saved and Israel shall dwell safely: and this is his name whereby he shall be called, The Lord Our Righteousness" (Jeremiah 23:5–6).

Elder Bruce R. McConkie quotes these verses along with several others to show that Christ "is also called David, that he is a new David, an Eternal David, who shall reign forever on the throne of his ancient ancestor."[4]

A covenant of peace with the Lord
(Ezekiel 34:25–31)

And I will make with them a covenant of peace, and will cause the evil beasts to cease out of the land: and they shall dwell safely in the wilderness, and sleep in the woods. And I will make them and the places round about my hill a blessing; and I will cause the shower to come down in his season; there shall be showers of blessing. And the tree of the field shall yield her fruit, and the earth shall yield her increase, and they shall be safe in their land, and shall know that I am the Lord, when I have broken the bands of their yoke, and delivered them out of the hand of those that served themselves of them. And they shall no more be a prey to the heathen, neither shall the beast of the land devour them; but they shall dwell safely, and none shall make them afraid. And I will raise up for them a plant of renown, and they shall be no more consumed with hunger in the land, neither bear the shame of the heathen any more. Thus shall they know that I the Lord their God am with them, and that they, even the house of Israel, are my people, saith the Lord God. And ye my flock, the flock of my pasture, are men, and I am your God, saith the Lord God.

Following his quotation of Ezekiel 34:23–24, as mentioned in the previous section, Elder McConkie continued: "When that day [the reign of David] comes, 'I will make with them a covenant of peace,' the

Lord says, meaning they shall have again the fulness of the everlasting gospel. Then 'there shall be showers of blessing'; all Israel shall dwell safely and know that the Lord is their God (Ezekiel 34:22–31)."[5] On another occasion, Elder McConkie stated before quoting verse 31, "What is an elder? He is a shepherd, a shepherd serving in the sheepfold of the Good Shepherd."[6] Elder McConkie was relating the calling of Melchizedek Priesthood holders to being shepherds of the flock of modern-day Israel.

A prophecy against Mount Seir
(Ezekiel 35:1–15)

Moreover the word of the Lord came unto me, saying, Son of man, set thy face against mount Seir, and prophesy against it, and say unto it, Thus saith the Lord God; Behold, O mount Seir, I am against thee, and I will stretch out mine hand against thee, and I will make thee most desolate. I will lay thy cities waste, and thou shalt be desolate, and thou shalt know that I am the Lord. Because thou hast had a perpetual hatred, and hast shed the blood of the children of Israel by the force of the sword in the time of their calamity, in the time that their iniquity had an end: therefore, as I live, saith the Lord God, I will prepare thee unto blood, and blood shall pursue thee: sith thou hast not hated blood, even blood shall pursue thee. Thus will I make mount Seir most desolate, and cut off from it him that passeth out and him that returneth. And I will fill his mountains with his slain men: in thy hills, and in thy valleys, and in all thy rivers, shall they fall that are slain with the sword. I will make thee perpetual desolations, and thy cities shall not return: and ye shall know that I am the Lord. Because thou hast said, These two nations and these two countries shall be mine, and we will possess it; whereas the Lord was there: therefore, as I live, saith the Lord God, I will even do according to thine anger, and according to thine envy which thou hast used out of thy hatred against them; and I will make myself known among them, when I have judged thee. And thou shalt know that I am the Lord, and that I have heard all thy blasphemies which thou hast spoken against the mountains of Israel, saying, They are laid desolate, they are given us to consume. Thus with your mouth ye have boasted against me, and have multiplied your words against me: I have heard them. Thus saith the Lord God;

9

When the whole earth rejoiceth, I will make thee desolate. As thou didst rejoice at the inheritance of the house of Israel, because it was desolate, so will I do unto thee: thou shalt be desolate, O mount Seir, and all Idumea, even all of it: and they shall know that I am the Lord.

Since the preceding and the subsequent chapters speak of the latter-day restoration of the gospel, it appears that this chapter must speak of the same time period. Therefore, the people of Mount Seir represent the Arab nations of today. While the internal evidence seems clear, it should be remembered that these people are also descendants of Abraham and, although not the covenant line, they still have blessings promised to them through Abraham. These people will come to know that Jehovah is the Lord and will have the blessings of the gospel extended to them in some future day. "All Idumea, even all of it: and they shall know that I am the Lord" (35:15) perhaps refers to all the descendants of Esau and Ishmael, not all the world, as in Doctrine and Covenants 1:36.

Israel gathered from among the heathen
(Ezekiel 36:1-7)

Also, thou son of man, prophesy unto the mountains of Israel, and say, Ye mountains of Israel, hear the word of the Lord:

Thus saith the Lord God; Because the enemy hath said against you, Aha, even the ancient high places are ours in possession:

Therefore prophesy and say, Thus saith the Lord God; Because they have made you desolate, and swallowed you up on every side, that ye might be a possession unto the residue of the heathen, and ye are taken up in the lips of talkers, and are an infamy of the people:

Therefore, ye mountains of Israel, hear the word of the Lord God; Thus saith the Lord God to the mountains, and to the hills, to the rivers, and to the valleys, to the desolate wastes, and to the cities that are forsaken, which became a prey and derision to the residue of the heathen that are round about;

Therefore thus saith the Lord God; Surely in the fire of my jealousy have I spoken against the residue of the heathen, and against all Idumea, which have appointed my land into their possession with the joy of all their heart, with despiteful minds, to cast it out for a prey.

Prophesy therefore concerning the land of Israel, and say unto the mountains, and to the hills, to the rivers, and to the valleys, Thus saith the Lord God; Behold, I have spoken in my jealousy and in my fury, because ye have borne the shame of the heathen:

Therefore thus saith the Lord God; I have lifted up mine hand, Surely the heathen that are about you, they shall bear their shame.

The residue of the heathen who swallowed up the house of Israel are the Gentiles who inhabited the mountains of Israel, or the Americas. Jacob, brother of Nephi, in commenting upon Isaiah, declared, "But behold, this land, said God, shall be a land of thine inheritance, and the Gentiles shall be blessed upon the land. And this land shall be a land of liberty unto the Gentiles, and there shall be no kings upon the land, who shall raise up unto the Gentiles" (2 Nephi 10:10–11).

Mormon, speaking of the downfall of the Nephite people, also recognized that the Gentiles would occupy this land: "And behold, the Lord hath reserved their blessings, which they might have received in the land, for the Gentiles who shall possess the land. But behold, it shall come to pass that they shall be driven and scattered by the Gentiles; and after they have been driven and scattered by the Gentiles, behold, then will the Lord remember the covenant which he made unto Abraham and unto all the house of Israel" (Mormon 5:19–20). Note that the covenant made unto Abraham would be fulfilled after the Lamanites had been scattered and driven by the Gentiles. This is consistent with Ezekiel 34:25, the "covenant of peace" enabling Israel to "dwell safely in the wilderness." Joseph Smith was designated by the Lord to be the one through whom Abraham's covenant would be fulfilled (D&C 124:58).

The Gentiles, however, will not take full advantage of the blessings reserved for them in the land of America and will "bear their shame" (Ezekiel 36:7) for their iniquity.

The mountains of Israel yield fruit
(Ezekiel 36:8–15)

But ye, O mountains of Israel, ye shall shoot forth your branches, and yield your fruit to my people of Israel; for they are at hand to come. For, behold, I am for you, and I will turn unto you, and ye shall be tilled and sown:

And I will multiply men upon you, all the house of Israel, even all of it: and the cities shall be inhabited, and the wastes shall be builded:

And I will multiply upon you man and beast; and they shall increase and bring fruit: and I will settle you after your old estates, and will do better unto you than at your beginnings; and ye shall know that I am the Lord.

Yea, I will cause men to walk upon you, even my people Israel; and they shall possess thee, and thou shalt be their inheritance, and thou shalt no more henceforth bereave them of men.

Thus saith the Lord God; Because they say unto you, Thou land devourest up men, and hast bereaved thy nations;

Therefore thou shalt devour men no more, neither bereave thy nations any more, saith the Lord God.

Neither will I cause men to hear in thee the shame of the heathen any more, neither shalt thou bear the reproach of the people any more, neither shalt thou cause thy nations to fall any more, saith the Lord God.

The cities being inhabited and waste places being built was also foretold by Isaiah (Isaiah 54:3; 61:4). In these verses, Isaiah prophesies about the latter days, as does Ezekiel in chapter 36. The cities will have become uninhabited from war, according to Isaiah 3:25–26 and Nephi's commentary on Isaiah 49 (1 Nephi 22:13–14). Israel will again possess the land as their inheritance (Ezekiel 36:12) and will overcome the Gentile culture that has been in the land (36:15; compare D&C 113:10; 84:54–58).

In answering questions on the writings of Isaiah, the Prophet Joseph Smith exclaimed that the loosing of the bands on the neck of the daughters, or inhabitants, of Zion (in America; see Isaiah 52:2) was "that the scattered remnants are exhorted to return to the Lord from whence they are fallen; which if they do, the promise of the Lord is that he will speak to them, or give them revelation. See the 6th, 7th, and 8th verses. The bands of her neck are the curses of God upon her, or the remnants of Israel in their scattered condition among the Gentiles" (D&C 113:10).

In other words, gathered Israel must live by revelation rather than follow the pattern of living set by the Gentiles among whom they are living. In another modern-day revelation, given two and one-half years after the Church was restored, the Lord chastised the Saints for treating "lightly the things you have received—which vanity and unbelief have brought the whole church under condemnation" (D&C 84:54–55). He then gave the solution to overcome the condemnation: "Repent and remember the new covenant, even the Book of Mormon and the former commandments which I have given them, not only to say, but to do according to that which I have written" (v. 57).

President Ezra Taft Benson renewed that challenge to the Church in October 1986 general conference (see "The Book of Mormon—Keystone of our Religion," Ensign, November 1986, 4–5).

Modern revelation also confirms that the remnant of Jacob, or the Lamanites, will rise up against the Gentiles. "And it shall come to pass also that the remnants who are left of the land will marshal themselves, and shall become exceedingly angry, and shall vex the Gentiles with a sore vexation" (D&C 87:5). The remnants of the land are, more particularly but not exclusively, the natives of Central and South America, where much unrest has periodically been shown against their governments.

Daniel H. Wells, a member of the First Presidency for twenty years (1857–1877), made this observation: "It appears more improbable, now, to the people of the United States, that the Indians should ever become so powerful an enemy and so dreadful a scourge to them, they would ever engage in so dreadful a civil war as that now raging. Yet this will as surely be fulfilled as have the other portions of this prophecy."[7]

To "cause men to walk upon you, even my people Israel" (Ezekiel 36:12) is probably the same prophecy as made by Micah (5:8–15) and quoted by the Savior to the Nephites, saying, "My people who are a remnant of Jacob shall be among the Gentiles . . . who . . . both treadeth down and teareth in pieces, and none can deliver" (3 Nephi 21:12; see also 21:13–21).

The Lord's name sanctified
(Ezekiel 36:16–23)

Moreover the word of the Lord came unto me, saying, Son of man, when the house of Israel dwelt in their own land, they defiled it by their own way and by their doings: their way was before me as the uncleanness of a removed woman.

Wherefore I poured my fury upon them for the blood that they had shed upon the land, and for their idols wherewith they had polluted it:

And I scattered them among the heathen, and they were dispersed through the countries: according to their way and according to their doings I judged them.

And when they entered unto the heathen, whither they went, they profaned my holy name, when they said to them, These are the people of the Lord, and are gone forth out of his land.

But I had pity for mine holy name, which the house of Israel had profaned among the heathen, whither they went.

Therefore say unto the house of Israel, Thus saith the Lord God; I do not this for your sakes, O house of Israel, but for mine holy name's sake, which ye have profaned among the heathen, whither ye went.

And I will sanctify my great name, which was profaned among the heathen, which ye have profaned in the midst of them; and the heathen shall know that I am the Lord, saith the Lord God, when I shall be sanctified in you before their eyes.

Because a new revelation begins in verse 16, it appears that the subject switches from the mountains of Israel in America to all of Israel being gathered. Therefore, the verses that follow have dual application. The people of Israel will gather to both America and Jerusalem, as evidenced by Jesus quoting Isaiah 52:8 as being fulfilled with both places and both peoples (3 Nephi 16:16–20; 20:32–35).

A new heart and a new spirit
(Ezekiel 36:24–29)

For I will take you from among the heathen, and gather you out of all countries, and will bring you into your own land. Then will I sprinkle clean water upon you, and ye shall be clean: from all your filthiness, and from all your idols, will I cleanse you. A new heart also will I give you, and a new spirit will I put within you: and I will take away the stony heart out of your flesh, and I will give you an heart of flesh. And I will put my spirit within you, and cause you to walk in my statutes, and ye shall keep my judgments, and do them. And ye shall dwell in the land that I gave to your fathers; and ye shall be my people, and I will be your God. I will also save you from all your uncleannesses: and I will call for the corn, and will increase it, and lay no famine upon you.

Elder McConkie, in his writings, has commented several times on these verses:

> If there is one recurring theme in all the prophecies relative to the gathering of Israel, it is that the new Israel will have a new heart and a new spirit and will keep the commandments; it is that they will receive the everlasting covenant, becoming thus the Lord's people, he being also their God; it is that they will be saved with an everlasting salvation because they become again as their ancient fathers once were. "I will take you from among the heathen, and gather you out of all countries, and will bring you into your own land," saith the Lord. After gathered Israel has come where the temple of God is, "Then will I sprinkle clean water upon you, and ye shall be clean: from all your filthiness, and from all your idols, will I cleanse you." Those with understanding will know the meaning of this. "A new heart also will I give you, and a new spirit will I put within you: and I will take away the stony heart out of your flesh, and I will give you an heart of flesh. And I will put my spirit within you, and cause you to walk in my statutes, and ye shall keep my judgments, and do them. And ye shall dwell in the land that I gave to your fathers; and ye shall be my people, and I will be your God. I will also save you from all your uncleanness" (Ezekiel 36:24–29).
>
> What greater blessings could there be than these? In the true sense they embrace all things. The Lord be praised for the gathering of his people![8]

On another occasion he wrote:

> A temple is also a sanctuary to which those who are striving with all their hearts to become like the Holy One may come to enter into sacred covenants with him. It is the place where baptisms for the dead are performed; where the faithful are endowed with power from on high; where the sealing power restored by Elijah unites worthy couples in the bonds of eternal matrimony; where the fulness of the priesthood is received;

and where those who are true and faithful in all things receive the assurance of eternal life in the Eternal Presence. A temple is a place where the Saints make the same covenants made by Abraham and receive for themselves the promises made to the fathers.

Thus, the Lord, as Ezekiel records, said to scattered Israel:

"I will take you from among the heathen, and gather you out of all countries, and bring you into your own land. Then will I sprinkle clean water upon you [in the holy temples] and ye shall be clean. . . ."

Truly, temples prepare a people to meet their God.[9]

On another occasion Elder McConkie, under the caption "Ordinances of the House of the Lord," said that verse 25 "has reference to the same things as do the words of revelation that say: 'Cleanse your hands and your feet before me, that I may make you clean; that I may testify unto your Father, and your God, and my God, that you are clean from the blood of this wicked generation' (Ezekiel 36:25; D&C 88:74–75)."[10]

The waste cities to be filled
(Ezekiel 36:30–38)

And I will multiply the fruit of the tree, and the increase of the field, that ye shall receive no more reproach of famine among the heathen.

Then shall ye remember your own evil ways, and your doings that were not good, and shall lothe yourselves in your own sight for your iniquities and for your abominations.

Not for your sakes do I this, saith the Lord God, be it known unto you: be ashamed and confounded for your own ways, O house of Israel.

Thus saith the Lord God; In the day that I shall have cleansed you from all your iniquities I will also cause you to dwell in the cities, and the wastes shall be builded.

And the desolate land shall be tilled, whereas it lay desolate in the sight of all that passed by. And they shall say, This land that was desolate is become like the garden of Eden; and the waste and desolate and ruined cities are become fenced, and are inhabited.

Then the heathen that are left round about you shall know

that I the Lord build the ruined places, and plant that that was desolate: I the Lord have spoken it, and I will do it.

Thus saith the Lord God; I will yet for this be enquired of by the house of Israel, to do it for them; I will increase them with men like a flock.

As the holy flock, as the flock of Jerusalem in her solemn feasts; so shall the waste cities be filled with flocks of men: and they shall know that I am the Lord.

Elder Parley P. Pratt interpreted 36:35–36 to apply to Jerusalem:

In the 36th chapter you will discover a promise, that Israel is to return from all nations whither they have been scattered, and to be brought again to the land which God gave to their fathers; Jerusalem is to be filled with flocks of men, and all the desolate cities of Judah are to be rebuilt, fenced, and inhabited; the land is to be fenced, tilled, and sown, insomuch that they shall say "this land that was desolate is become like the garden of Eden" . . . "the heathen shall know that I the Lord build the ruined places, and plant that which is desolate. So shall the waste cities be filled with flocks of men, and they shall know that I am the Lord.[11]

The blessing of building cities and waste places has certainly happened in Palestine. The Prophet Joseph Smith changed "plant that that was desolate" in verse 36 to "plant that which was desolate" (JST, Ezekiel 36:36), an insignificant change but more readable. Verse 37 implies the whole house of Israel will inquire of the Lord, not just part of it. Also, verse 38 is a comparison to "the flock of Jerusalem in her solemn feasts," not a designation of where it will take place.

Summary of Chapters 34–36

In modern scripture, Jesus identifies himself as "the good shepherd and the stone of Israel. He that buildeth upon this rock shall never fail" (D&C 50:44; compare Genesis 49:24). Such a designation certainly confirms the interpretation of the shepherd in Ezekiel chapter 34 being the Lord Jesus Christ. His work of gathering, foretold by Ezekiel, is well underway. His covenant of peace (34:25) and many of his temples, or "sanctuaries" (see 37:26), have been established. The process for obtaining a new heart and a new spirit is offered to all who will come follow the voice of the shepherd. The gathering has proceeded much further in the Americas than in Mount Seir and the area of Palestine, but that will come in the near future. As it comes, the separation of the "cattle and the cattle" (34:17), or the cleansing of the Church (see D&C 112:23–26; Matthew 13:47–50), will also come. It will probably happen in a very natural way without those who become separated fully realizing what is happening to them. Ezekiel's prophecies of the Restoration are coming to pass, and those who are gathered now "know that I the Lord their God am with them" (Ezekiel 34:30). They are gathering to the land that was given to their fathers and fulfilling the prophecy that "ye shall be my people, and I will be your God" (36:28; compare Exodus 6:7). Furthermore, as Ezekiel repeatedly says, all people will soon "know that I am the Lord" (35:15; 36:11, 23, 36, 38).

Notes

1. Joseph Smith, *Teachings of the Prophet Joseph Smith*, sel. Joseph Fielding Smith (Salt Lake City: Deseret Book, 1976), 315.
2. Ibid., 17.
3. Ibid., 102.
4. Bruce R. McConkie, *The Promised Messiah* (Salt Lake City: Deseret Book, 1978), 193–94.
5. Ibid., 194–95; see also Joseph Fielding Smith, *The Way to Perfection* (Salt Lake City: Genealogical Society of The Church of Jesus Christ of Latter-day Saints, 1953), 311.
6. Bruce R. McConkie, "Only an Elder," *Ensign*, June 1975, 66.
7. Daniel H. Wells, in Roy W. Doxey, *Latter-day Prophets and the Doctrine and Covenants*, 4 vols. (Salt Lake City: Deseret Book, 1963–65), 3:148–49.
8. ———, *A New Witness for the Articles of Faith* (Salt Lake City: Deseret Book, 1985), 553.
9. ———, *The Millennial Messiah* (Salt Lake City: Deseret Book, 1982), 273.
10. ———, *The Mortal Messiah* (Salt Lake City: Deseret Book, 1979), 1:105.
11. Parley P. Pratt, *"Voice of Warning,"* as quoted in Joseph Fielding Smith, *The Progress of Man* (Salt Lake City: Deseret Book, 1973), 404–5.

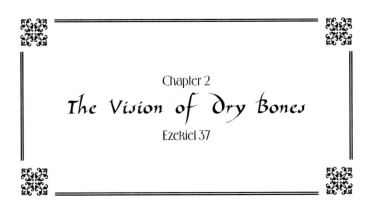

Chapter 2

The Vision of Dry Bones

Ezekiel 37

oes the Bible foretell the coming forth of the Book of Mormon? The answer to this question is a definite yes! Such passages as Isaiah 29, Ezekiel 37, Psalm 85, and Revelation 14 are commonly cited to support that answer. Is the interpretation of these references justified? Again, yes! Only an analysis of Ezekiel 37 will be given here, but similar support could be given for the other passages referred to above.

Because of these two questions, the most widely quoted chapter in the book of Ezekiel in Latter-day Saint literature is undoubtedly the 37th. While verses fifteen through seventeen are the most quoted verses, the whole chapter is of extreme importance to the latter-day Restoration. It begins with a vision shown to Ezekiel and a conversation between him and the Lord God. The Lord commands Ezekiel to prophesy and Ezekiel obeys. A revelation to Ezekiel follows. The entire chapter is outlined below.

1. Ezekiel 37:1–14. Ezekiel is carried by the spirit of the Lord into an open valley full of very dry bones.
   a. The Lord asks if the bones can live; Ezekiel says the Lord knows (37:3).
   b. The Lord tells Ezekiel to prophesy that the Lord

will cause the bones to live and they shall know he is the Lord (37:4–6).

   c. Ezekiel prophesies, and the bones come together with sinews and flesh, but there is no breath in them (37:7–8).

   d. The Lord tells Ezekiel to prophesy to the wind. The wind is to come from the four winds and breathe upon the slain that they may live (37:9).

   e. Ezekiel prophesies as commanded, and the slain become an exceeding great army (37:10).

   f. The Lord identifies the bones as the whole house of Israel. The Lord tells Ezekiel to prophesy that the Lord will open their graves and put His spirit in them and bring them to their own land (37:11–14).

2. Ezekiel 37:15–28. A revelation comes to Ezekiel telling him to take one stick and write upon it for Judah, and another stick and write upon it for Joseph. He is then to join them together into one stick, and they shall become one in his hand.

   a. When the children ask the meaning of the revelation, the Lord tells Ezekiel to say the Lord will take the stick, which is in the hand of Ephraim, and put it with the stick of Judah. They will become one stick before their eyes (37:18–20).

   b. The Lord tells Ezekiel to say the Lord will gather the children of Israel from among the heathen and make them one nation in the land upon the mountains of Israel, and one king shall be over them all. They will not be two nations or be defiled anymore (37:21–23).

   c. David, the Lord's servant, shall be king over them. They shall have one shepherd and dwell in the land given to Jacob (37:24–25).

   d. The Lord will make an everlasting covenant of peace with Israel and set his sanctuary in the midst of them evermore; the heathen will know the Lord does sanctify Israel (37:26–28).

Notes and Commentary

In this chapter, the Lord uses the resurrection of the body to symbolize the gathering of all the house of Israel. The overall message is that the promised restoration of the house of Israel will be brought to pass, and this will be the emphases in our discussion of Ezekiel 37. There are many of the brethren who have quoted the middle verses to show the coming forth of the Book of Mormon. Many of these quotes are repetitions, so only a few of them will be used. The latter verses are less quoted, but there are several quotes that show the complete restoration of the kingdom of Israel with its temple building as the ultimate objective of the kingdom.

The Prophet Joseph Smith made no changes in this chapter in his translation of the Bible, nor did Joseph specifically use this chapter to teach of latter-day temples, although he taught much about temple building and its importance.

Many significant evidences that clarify the interpretation of this chapter have been furnished by Latter-day Saint scholars using some of the more recent findings regarding Ezekiel's use of ancient terminology such as "stick." However, there is little agreement among Bible scholars in general regarding the interpretation of these verses collectively.

The valley of dry bones
(Ezekiel 37:1-2)

The hand of the Lord was upon me, and carried me out in the spirit of the Lord, and set me down in the midst of the valley which was full of bones, and caused me to pass by them round about: and, behold, there were very many in the open valley; and, lo, they were very dry.

The place that Ezekiel was carried is not given. It is assumed that it was a place where a large number of the house of Israel had once lived or had been killed by warfare or some other means. The description of the bones being "very dry" (37:2) indicates they had been lying there a long time. The designation of the place was obviously not important for the Lord to teach his lesson to Ezekiel.

Can these dry bones live?
(Ezekiel 37:3-10)

And he said unto me, Son of man, can these bones live? And I answered, O Lord God, thou knowest. Again he said unto me, Prophesy upon these bones, and say unto them, O ye dry bones, hear the word of the Lord.

Thus saith the Lord God unto these bones; Behold, I will cause breath to enter into you, and ye shall live: And I will lay sinews upon you, and will bring up flesh upon you, and cover you with skin, and put breath in you, and ye shall live; and ye shall know that I am the Lord.

So I prophesied as I was commanded: and as I prophesied, there was a noise, and behold a shaking, and the bones came together, bone to his bone.

And when I beheld, lo, the sinews and the flesh came up upon them, and the skin covered them above: but there was no breath in them.

Then said he unto me, Prophesy unto the wind, prophesy, son of man, and say to the wind, Thus saith the Lord God; Come from the four winds, O breath, and breathe upon these slain, that they may live.

So I prophesied as he commanded me, and the breath came into them, and they lived, and stood up upon their feet, an exceeding great army.

Ezekiel's answer to the Lord's question, "can these bones live?" (37:3), exemplifies his faith. He acknowledges that the Lord knows and implies that only the Lord knows the mysteries, or things that have not yet been revealed. Since the resurrection had not occurred, it was more of a mystery in the day of Ezekiel than today, although it is still a mystery to most. While there were many people resurrected at the time of Christ (Matthew 27:52–53; 3 Nephi 23:9–10), the concept of a literal resurrection is still not generally taught in the Christian world and, thus, remains a mystery.

The coming together of the bones, the sinews, and the flesh, as prophesied by and shown to Ezekiel, is apparently how the body will be resurrected when the time comes. That the body was still not alive until the breath entered it shows that the Spirit entering the body is the final stage of resurrection. The breath coming from the four winds apparently represents the spirits coming from Paradise to reclaim their bodies. Thus, the eternal principles of the literal resurrection are certainly taught, as the early latter-day brethren emphasized.

Elder Orson Pratt explained, "When the Lord brings up the children of Israel out of their graves, he will do it just as Ezekiel saw it in vision. The materials that form the bones will come together: first, the anatomy or framework, the most part of the system; then the flesh; afterwards the skin; and then the Spirit of the living God will enter into them, and they will live as immortal beings, no more to be subject to death.[1]

Israel to be gathered to their own lands
(Ezekiel 37:11-14)

Then he said unto me, Son of man, these bones are the whole house of Israel: behold, they say, Our bones are dried, and our hope is lost: we are cut off for our parts. Therefore prophesy and say unto them, Thus saith the Lord God; Behold, O my people, I will open your graves, and cause you to come up out of your graves, and bring you into the land of Israel.

And ye shall know that I am the Lord, when I have opened your graves, O my people, and brought you up out of your graves, And shall put my spirit in you, and ye shall live, and I shall place you in your own land: then shall ye know that I the Lord have spoken it, and performed it, saith the Lord.

In this section, the Lord's interpretation of the preceding verses is given. The principles of the resurrection were used to show Ezekiel that the whole house of Israel at this time were widely dispersed, but they would be gathered again to their lands promised to them by the Lord. There is probably a dual message involved here; first, the faithful members of the house of Israel who have passed away from the earth will be literally resurrected and become a part of the celestial earth in the eternal scheme of the Lord. Second, the context of this chapter is that all the house of Israel (or their descendants)—the ten tribes who had been dispersed into the north, the Nephites who had been taken away, the Jews who were captive in Babylon and scattered to the ends of the earth, and all the rest who were scattered in other places—would be gathered to the lands of Israel. In these verses, the Lord tells Ezekiel what is going to happen in the future. He next tells him how he will bring about the gathering.

The sticks of Judah and Ephraim
(Ezekiel 37:15-17)

The word of the Lord came again unto me, saying, Moreover, thou son of man, take thee one stick, and write upon it, For Judah, and for the children of Israel his companions: then take another stick, and write upon it, For Joseph, the stick of Ephraim, and for all the house of Israel his companions: and join them one to another into one stick; and they shall become one in thine hand.

The two sticks being brought together are interpreted by the Latter-day Saints to be the Book of Mormon coming forth and being joined with the Bible. The testimony of President Wilford Woodruff is typical of many: "Joseph Smith was raised up by the power of God, and the administration of angels, and he brought forth the Book of Mormon, the record and stick of Joseph in the hands of Ephraim, as spoken of by the Prophet Ezekiel in the 37th chapter."[2] Many modern-day apostles have further qualified the interpretation of the sticks. Elder Boyd K. Packer stated:

> The sticks, of course, are records or books. In ancient Israel records were written upon tablets of wood or scrolls rolled upon sticks. The record of Judah and the record of Ephraim, according to the prophecy, were to become one in our hands.[3]

President Brigham Young also made this identification:

> The Old and New Testaments are the stick of Judah. You recollect that the tribe of Judah tarried in Jerusalem and the Lord blessed Judah, and the result was the writings of the Old and New Testaments. But where is the stick of Joseph? Can you tell where it is? Yes. It was the children of Joseph who came across the waters to this continent, and this land was filled with people, and the Book of Mormon or the stick of Joseph contains their writings, and they are in the hands of Ephraim. Where are the Ephraimites? They are mixed through all the nations of the earth. God is calling upon them to gather out, and He is uniting them, and they are giving the Gospel to the whole world.[4]

The writing upon scrolls rolled on sticks has long been one of the accepted record-keeping methods. However, writing upon wooden tablets has more recently been discovered. Wooden tablets were discovered and reported to the academic world in 1948. These tablets were discovered in ancient southern Babylonia, the area where Ezekiel was in captivity. *The New English Bible*, a translation sponsored by the Protestant churches and Bible societies in the British Isles, translates Ezekiel 37:15–20 as follows:

> These were the words of the Lord to me: Man, take one leaf of a wooden tablet and write on it, "Judah and his associates of Israel." Then take another leaf and write on it, "Joseph, the leaf

of Ephraim and all his associates of Israel." Now bring the two together to form one tablet; then they will be a folding tablet in your hand. When your fellow-countrymen ask you to tell them what you mean by this, say to them, These are the words of the Lord God: I am taking the leaf of Joseph, which belongs to Ephraim and his associate tribes of Israel, and joining to it the leaf of Judah. Thus I shall make them one tablet, and they shall be one in my hand. The leaves on which you shall write shall be visible in your hand for all to see.[5]

Another discovery of the last century also supports the concept of Ezekiel's two sticks being records. Hugh Nibley has written about this discovery.

> Ezekiel is in all probability here referring to an institution which flourished among the ancient Hebrews but was completely lost sight of after the Middle Ages until its rediscovery in the last century. That is the institution of the tally-sticks. A tally is "a stick notched and split through the notches, so that both parties to a transaction may have a part of the record." That is, when a contract was made certain official marks were placed upon a stick of wood in the presence of a notary representing the king. The marks indicated the nature of the contract, what goods and payments were involved, and the names of the contracting parties. Then the stick was split down the middle, and each of the parties kept half as his claim-token (hence our word "stock" from "stick") and his check upon the other party (hence called a "foil"). Now both parties possessed a sure means of identification and an authoritative claim upon each other no matter how many miles or how many years might separate them. For the tally-stick was fool-proof. When the time for settlement came and the king's magistrate placed the two sticks side by side to see that all was in order, the two would only fit together perfectly mark for mark and grain for grain to "become one" in the King's hand if they had been one originally—no two other halves in the world would match without a flaw; and if either of the parties had attempted to add or efface any item of the bill (bill means originally also a stick of wood), by putting any new marks or "indentures" upon it the fraud would become at once apparent. So when the final payment was made and all the terms of the contract fulfilled, the two pieces of wood were joined by the King's magistrate at the exchequer, tied as one, and laid up

forever in the royal vaults, becoming as it were "one in the king's hand."[6]

Both Keith Meservy ("Ezekiel's Sticks" *Ensign*, September 1977, 22–27) and Nibley point out that the Hebrew word translated as "stick" means "wood," and, as Nibley points out, its interpretation depends on how it is used. Thus, scientific discoveries are sustaining the LDS interpretation of Ezekiel 37:15–17.

Ezekiel was not the only prophet who foretold the keeping of two records. As quoted by Lehi, Joseph of Egypt made a similar prophecy while still in Egypt.

> But a seer will I raise up out of the fruit of thy loins; and unto him will I give power to bring forth my word unto the seed of thy loins—and not to the bringing forth my word only, saith the Lord, but to the convincing them of my word, which shall have already gone forth among them.
>
> Wherefore, the fruit of thy loins shall write; and the fruit of the loins of Judah shall write; and that which shall be written by the fruit of thy loins, and also that which shall be written by the fruit of the loins of Judah, shall grow together, unto the confounding of false doctrines and laying down of contentions, and establishing peace among the fruit of thy loins, and bringing them to the knowledge of their fathers in the latter days, and also to the knowledge of my covenants, saith the Lord. (2 Nephi 3:11–12)

The two records growing together is the same process as spoken of by Ezekiel, "becoming one in thine hand." While the two records may be physically held together in our hand or even published as one unit, there is also a spiritual unification of the two records. As they are studied together, our knowledge of the gospel increases; they "grow together" as two witnesses teaching the same gospel of Jesus Christ, thus accomplishing the purposes mentioned by the prophecy of Joseph of Egypt. One of the major purposes of the Book of Mormon is to prove the truthfulness of the Bible, thus "proving to the world that the holy scriptures are true" (D&C 20:11). Elder Orson Pratt observed:

> Now you see that this record of the tribe of Joseph, called the Book of Mormon, agrees in all its particulars, so far as doctrine is concerned, with the record of the tribe of Judah; hence the testimony of two nations should be a witness to all people,

nations and tongues respecting the truth of Christianity: and instead of doing away with Christianity, the Book of Mormon—the record or stick of Joseph, is an additional testimony to the great and important truths contained in the Bible; it is a testimony against the corruptions that have been introduced into the world under the name of Christianity.[7]

The stick of Joseph put with the stick of Judah (Ezekiel 37:18-20)

And when the children of thy people shall speak unto thee, saying, Wilt thou not shew us what thou meanest by these? Say unto them, Thus saith the Lord God; Behold, I will take the stick of Joseph, which is in the hand of Ephraim, and the tribes of Israel his fellows, and will put them with him, even with the stick of Judah, and make them one stick, and they shall be one in mine hand. And the sticks whereon thou writest shall be in thine hand before their eyes.

The Lord's instructions to Ezekiel are given for the benefit of generations to follow Ezekiel's time. Elder LeGrand Richards has written:

When this command was given, it was the equivalent of directing that two books or records should be kept. A careful reading will indicate that it would be in coming generations (v. 18), when their children would ask the meaning of this commandment, that the Lord would "take the stick of Joseph, which is in the hand of Ephraim, and the tribes of Israel his fellows, and will put them with him, even with the stick of Judah, and make them one stick, and they shall be one in mine hand."

Note that the Lord said he would do this and would make them one in his hand. Now, granting that the Bible is the stick of Judah, where is the stick of Joseph? Can anyone answer? God commanded that it should be kept to record the fulfillment of his greater promises to Joseph. It would naturally be a record kept in another land, since Joseph was to be "separate from his brethren." It is plain from the reading of this scripture that the record of Judah, or the Holy Bible, would remain with this people, that the record of Joseph would be joined unto it, and that the two would become one.

Should anyone object to God's doing exactly what he promised Ezekiel he would do? Could this promise be fulfilled in

27

a simpler and more perfect manner than it was through the coming forth of the Book of Mormon? God led a branch of the house of Joseph to America and commanded them to keep records of all their doings. He then commanded his prophet Moroni to hide this sacred record in the Hill Cumorah in the western part of the American state of New York. Centuries later he sent Moroni back to deliver the record to Joseph Smith, and gave Joseph power to translate it with the assistance of the Urim and Thummim. The two records have now been joined together, constituting a complete fulfillment of another great prophecy. Again, who could object to God's doing the thing he promised to do? Until someone can explain where the record of Joseph is, the Book of Mormon stands unrefuted in its claim to be "the stick of Joseph."[8]

That the stick of Joseph was to be in the hands of Ephraim is also significant. Ephraim, son of Joseph of Egypt, was the recipient of the birthright and, thus, had the responsibility of initiating the promised Restoration prophesied by Ezekiel (1 Chronicles 5:1–2; Jeremiah 31:9). Joseph Smith was from the tribe of Ephraim (see Joseph Fielding Smith, *Doctrines of Salvation*, 3:253–54). Moroni was sent to him to reveal the Book of Mormon: "Behold, this is wisdom in me; wherefore, marvel not, for the hour cometh that I will drink of the fruit of the vine with you on the earth, and with Moroni, whom I have sent unto you to reveal the Book of Mormon, containing the fulness of my everlasting gospel, to whom I have committed the keys of the record of the stick of Ephraim" (D&C 27:5; see also D&C 113:1–6).

The Book of Mormon being the stick of Ephraim was verified by Elder Harold B. Lee to Seminary and Institute teachers assembled at BYU in 1968. "Some teach, according to some reports . . . that the stick of Joseph does not refer to the Book of Mormon and that the Doctrine and Covenants, section 27, verse 5 which declares it to be is not to be taken literally. God forbid that any of you teachers will teach any such doctrine or allow it to be taught without a challenge from you who know the truth and have a testimony."[9] The coming forth of the Book of Mormon would then fulfill a prophecy of the Lord to Nephi:

> Wherefore murmur ye, because that ye shall receive more of my word? Know ye not that the testimony of two nations is a witness unto you that I am God, that I remember one nation like

unto another? Wherefore, I speak the same words unto one nation like unto another. And when the two nations shall run together the testimony of the two nations shall run together also.

And I do this that I may prove unto many that I am the same yesterday, today, and forever; and that I speak forth my words according to mine own pleasure. And because that I have spoken one word ye need not suppose that I cannot speak another; for my work is not yet finished; neither shall it be until the end of man, neither from that time henceforth and forever. (2 Nephi 29:8–9)

After the two nations or continents ran together, the Bible and the Book of Mormon came together, as told to Nephi. Perhaps Ezekiel was shown or told more than he wrote. Elder Bruce R. McConkie made this observation: "We wonder . . . if Ezekiel did not say more to the people than is here recorded. There is no reason why he should not have told them of the remnant of Joseph that escaped from Jerusalem."[10] Since Joseph of Egypt had prophesied of the two records nearly one thousand years earlier (2 Nephi 3:11–12), the existence of another record may well have been known and, thus, Ezekiel either did not mention it or it was deleted as suggested by Elder McConkie.

One nation in the mountains of Israel (Ezekiel 37:21–23)

And say unto them, Thus saith the Lord God; Behold, I will take the children of Israel from among the heathen, whither they be gone, and will gather them on every side, and bring them into their own land:

And I will make them one nation in the land upon the mountains of Israel; and one king shall be king to them all: and they shall be no more two nations, neither shall they be divided into two kingdoms any more at all:

Neither shall they defile themselves any more with their idols, nor with their detestable things, nor with any of their transgressions: but I will save them out of all their dwelling-places, wherein they have sinned, and will cleanse them: so shall they be my people, and I will be their God.

The interpretation of the prophecy as the gathering of Israel from among the heathen, or Gentiles, is a repeat of 34:11–14 and 36:24;

however, these verses add the dimension of Israel being one nation, not two kingdoms (northern ten tribes and southern Judah), with one king over them. Elder McConkie has written:

> Israel—all Israel, including those of the kingdom of Judah and those of the Kingdom of Israel, who are the ten tribes—shall gather, be one, and have one King. There is nothing mysterious or hidden or unknown as to how and why and in what manner Israel—all Israel—shall gather [quotes Jeremiah 3:14, 18]. The process of gathering is now and always will be one in which the scattered remnants of Jacob—those of all tribes—believe the Book of Mormon, accept the restored gospel, and come to the latter-day Zion, there to receive the same blessings that once were showered upon their fathers. This gathering will be one person here, and two there, and a few somewhere else—all by the power of a book, the stick of Joseph joined with the stick of Judah. When they gather and become one people, they will be a new and changed people [quotes Ezekiel 37:23]. They will believe in Christ, repent of their sins, be baptized for the remission of sins, and receive the gift of the Holy Ghost, thereby being cleansed and having their sins burned away as though by fire.[11]

In another publication, Elder McConkie wrote:

> This gathering is now in process and will continue until the two ancient kingdoms are fully established again [quotes Ezekiel 37:22]. The illustration used to teach the unity and oneness of this gathering is perfect. The two nations shall be one as the Bible and the Book of Mormon are one. No one who truly believes the Bible can reject the Book of Mormon, and every person who believes the Book of Mormon believes also the Bible. They speak with one voice. And so shall it be with the two kingdoms of Israel. They will be perfectly united in the last days, believing the same truths, walking in the same paths, worshiping the same Lord, and glorying in the same eternal covenants [quotes from Ezekiel 37:23]. False worship shall cease where they are concerned. As their fathers rejected Baal, so they shall forsake the creeds of Christendom that exhort men to worship an incomprehensible spirit nothingness to which the names of Deity have been given. No more will they walk in the ways of the world; no more will they wallow in the mire of Babylon;

no more will they delight in the passions and lusts of carnal men [quotes from Ezekiel 37:23]. Their sins will be washed away in the waters of baptism; they will be born again; and they will become the children of Christ, his sons and his daughters.[12]

Elder Orson Pratt asked a pertinent question about the prophesied gathering of the house of Israel and then gave an answer.

Has this been fulfilled? Has He done this for the House of Israel, scattered among the heathen, bringing them back and making them one nation in the land and upon the mountains, with one king to reign over them all? Has there ever been a period since the twelve tribes lived, some two thousand five hundred years ago, that the House of Judah has been made one? It is very well known that such things have not yet taken place. But the prophecy will be fulfilled, and that too in our day. The Lord will gather the ten tribes from the north, and the House of Judah from the four quarters of the earth whither they be gone, and will gather them on every side, and bring them into their own land, making of them one nation under one king never more to be divided, neither, says the Lord, shall they any more defile themselves with their detestable things, etc.[13]

David my servant, the king
(Ezekiel 37:24-25)

And David my servant shall be king over them; and they all shall have one shepherd: they shall also walk in my judgments, and observe my statutes, and do them. And they shall dwell in the land that I have given unto Jacob my servant, wherein your fathers have dwelt; and they shall dwell therein, even they, and their children, and their children's children for ever: and my servant David shall be their prince for ever.

The king is identified as "David my servant." As explained earlier, this has reference to Jesus Christ, a descendant of King David, who was promised his throne would be established forever (see 2 Samuel 7:16). Again we turn to Elder McConkie to add another witness that the David spoken of by Ezekiel is Jesus Christ.

What David? The Eternal David, the Lord Our Righteousness, who shall dwell among his people and reign in power and glory over all the earth. "And they shall have one shepherd." What Shepherd? The Good Shepherd, the Lord Jehovah, who led their fathers anciently and will now lead them in the same paths. "For there is one God and one Shepherd over all the earth" (1 Nephi 13:41). And "they shall also walk in my judgments, and observe my statutes, and do them." They shall keep the commandments, even as the people did in the Zion of old, when once before the Lord came and dwelt with his people and they dwelt in righteousness.[14]

Elder McConkie also identified where the children of Israel would dwell as the subjects of King David.

> And where shall they dwell? In the land given unto Jacob, old Canaan, the Jewish Palestine, the Holy Land where also our Lord lived during mortality. And how long shall they abide there? They and their children, and their children's children, shall dwell there forever. The meek shall inherit the earth. This is not to say that there are not other lands of promise, and that the American land of Joseph shall not become the inheritance of Nephites and that portion of latter-day Israel, in the main, which is now in the restored kingdom; but it is to say that the Israel of Ezekiel's day, which was Jewish, shall dwell in the land of old Jerusalem, where their temple will be built.[15]

When will this nation be established? Jesus taught that "Jerusalem shall be trodden down of the Gentiles, until the times of the Gentiles be fulfilled" (Luke 21:24; see also JST, Luke 21:24–26). Another account of that same sermon, which was revealed to the Prophet Joseph Smith, is found in the Doctrine and Covenants:

> And this I have told you concerning Jerusalem; and when that day shall come, shall a remnant be scattered among all nations; but they shall be gathered again; but they shall remain until the times of the Gentiles be fulfilled. And in that day shall be heard of wars and rumors of wars, and the whole earth shall be in commotion, and men's hearts shall fail them, and they shall say that Christ delayeth his coming until the end of the earth. And the love of men shall wax cold, and iniquity shall abound. And when the times of the Gentiles is come in, a light shall break forth among them that sit in darkness, and it shall be the fulness of my gospel; but they receive it not; for they perceive not the light, and they turn their hearts from me because of the

precepts of men. And in that generation shall the times of the Gentiles be fulfilled. (D&C 45:24–30)

We are living in the times of the Gentiles, and the conditions prevalent when the times of the Gentiles would be fulfilled are fast approaching (see 3 Nephi 16:10–11). While we do not know the Lord's exact timetable, we can recognize his signs. Although those signs show unrest and troublesome times, there will be internal peace among the righteous as well as future external peace. Ezekiel also foretold of this time period.

An everlasting covenant of peace
(Ezekiel 37:26–28)

Moreover I will make a covenant of peace with them; it shall be an everlasting covenant with them: and I will place them, and multiply them, and will set my sanctuary in the midst of them for evermore. My tabernacle also shall be with them: yea, I will be their God, and they shall be my people. And the heathen shall know that I the Lord do sanctify Israel, when my sanctuary shall be in the midst of them for evermore.

The "covenant of peace" is the everlasting covenant of the gospel (see D&C 45:9). The sanctuary and the tabernacle in these verses of Ezekiel refer to the temple, as Elder McConkie states:

The covenant of peace, the everlasting covenant is the gospel—the gospel of the Lord Jesus Christ, the gospel restored through Joseph Smith and his associates. It contains that plan of salvation which requires the building of temples so that all the ordinances of salvation and exaltation may be performed for the living and the dead. In the very nature of things the Lord's sanctuary, his temple, will stand in the midst of his congregations; otherwise they would not be his people. We have, then, an express prophecy of the building of the Lord's sanctuary, not alone in Jackson County where the New Jerusalem will be built, but in Old Jerusalem, in the land of Judah, among and for the people who descended from those who worshiped there in Solomon's Temple, in Zerubbabel's Temple, and in Herod's Temple.[16]

On another occasion Elder McConkie wrote:

In that day all Israel, gathered in from their long dispersion, shall receive the everlasting covenant, which is in the everlasting gospel. The Lord's temple shall be in their midst, wherein the other tribes shall come to Ephraim to receive their blessings, according to the promises. There will also be tabernacles of assembly wherein the people will worship. And all men will know that the Lord has fulfilled his promises to Israel, that they are his people and he is their God.

And it will all be brought to pass by a book—the Book of Mormon—and by the restoration to them of the same gospel in which their forebears rejoiced.[17]

Summary of Chapter 37

Ezekiel 37 is a prophecy of the coming forth of the Book of Mormon and also of other events associated with the restoration of the gospel in the latter days. This is confirmed to us by many witnesses: new translations of the Bible giving more exact wording of the text, discovery of ancient practices sustaining the meaning of the prophecy, the prophecies of old quoted in the Book of Mormon, and, most importantly, the interpretation of modern Apostles.

Through the coming forth of the Book of Mormon, many temples have been built and many more will be built. Much of Ezekiel 37 has come to pass and much more is happening now. We should appreciate what the Lord has shown to Ezekiel and anxiously anticipate what is yet to come.

Notes

1. Orson Pratt, in *Journal of Discourses*, 26 vols. (London: Latter-day Saints' Book Depot, 1854–86), 19:290.

2. James R. Clark, *Messages of the First Presidency* (Salt Lake City: Bookcraft, 1966), 3:94.

3. Boyd K. Packer, "Scriptures," *Ensign,* November 1982, 51.

4. Brigham Young, in *Journal of Discourses*, 13:175.

5. *The New English Bible*, Ezekiel 37:15–20; see also Keith H. Meservy, "Ezekiel's Sticks," *Ensign*, September 1977, 22–27. This excellent article, too long for inclusion here, maintains that the word "sticks" used in the KJV translation is indeed a reference to records that were kept.

6. Hugh Nibley, *An Approach to the Book of Mormon*, 3rd ed. (Salt Lake City:

Deseret Book; Provo, Utah: The Foundation for Ancient Research and Mormon Studies, 1998), 319.

7. Orson Pratt, in *Journal of Discourses*, 16:350–51.

8. LeGrand Richards, *A Marvelous Work and a Wonder* (Salt Lake City: Deseret Book, 1976), 66–67.

9. Harold B. Lee, "Viewpoint of a Giant," unpublished talk given at Brigham Young University to seminary and institute teachers, July 18, 1968; copy in possession of the author.

10. Bruce R. McConkie, *A New Witness for the Articles of Faith* (Salt Lake City: Deseret Book, 1985), 456–57.

11. Ibid.

12. Bruce R. McConkie, *The Millennial Messiah* (Salt Lake City: Deseret Book, 1982), 606–7.

13. Orson Pratt, in *Journal of Discourses*, 19:173.

14. McConkie, *The Millennial Messiah*, 607.

15. Bruce R. McConkie, *The Mortal Messiah* (Salt Lake City: Deseret Book, 1979), 1:120.

16. Ibid., 1:120–21.

17. McConkie, *A New Witness for the Articles of Faith*, 458.

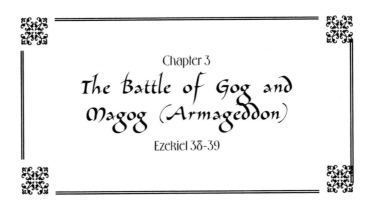

Chapter 3

The Battle of Gog and Magog (Armageddon)

Ezekiel 38–39

ne of the signs to precede Christ's Second Coming is that "you shall also hear of wars and rumors of war" (Joseph Smith—Matthew 1:23). The ultimate sign of these wars is the gathering of all nations against Jerusalem (Zechariah 13:2–5; Luke 21:20–24), or as Joel says, "Assemble yourselves, and come, all ye heathen . . . come up to the valley of Jehoshaphat. . . . Multitudes, multitudes in the valley of decision: for the day of the Lord is near in the valley of decision" (Joel 3:11, 12, 14). Ezekiel describes the war in these chapters as the battle of Gog and Magog.

The Prophet Joseph Smith said, "The battle of Gog and Magog will be after the millennium . . . the remnant of all the nations that fight against Jerusalem were commanded to go up to Jerusalem to worship in the millennium."[1] There is nothing else recorded to indicate the context of the Prophet's statement. It appears the Prophet was responding to a question or a comment. The second part of the Prophet's statement refers to a battle before the Millennium, but he did not call it the battle of Gog and Magog. However, the Book of Ezekiel also refers to the last great battle before the Second Coming as the battle of Gog and

Magog (see Ezekiel 38:2–3, 15–16). The New Testament calls this last great battle before the millennium Armageddon (Revelation 16:16). The Gog and Magog battle at the end of the millennium spoken of by the Prophet in the quotation above is spoken of in Revelation 20:7–10. We will discuss the battle of Gog and Magog in Ezekiel's terms.

Ezekiel's description of the great battle before the Millennium shows the destruction of the wicked before and during the Second Coming. It is the downfall of Satan and his forces. Although Ezekiel does not give a lot of detail, what he does say is outlined below.

1. Ezekiel 38:1–13. The Lord is against Gog, the chief prince of Meshech and Tubal in the land of Magog.
   a. The Lord will turn all the nations back and many people with them (38:4–6).
   b. The nations are warned to be prepared (38:7).
   c. In the latter years, Gog will come into the land where the gathering out of nations has taken place to spoil them (38:8–13).
2. Ezekiel 38:14–23. A prophecy to Gog in the latter days. When the Lord brings him against the people of Israel, the Lord will be sanctified in Gog before the eyes of Israel.
   a. There will be a great shaking in the land of Israel, all the beasts and the men shall shake at the Lord's presence (38:17–20).
   b. Every man's sword will be against his brother, and the Lord will plead against Gog with pestilence, blood, hailstones, fire, and brimstones (38:21–22).
   c. The Lord will be sanctified and known in the eyes of many nations (38:23).
3. Ezekiel 39:1–7. A prophecy against Gog. The Lord will turn Gog back and leave but the sixth part of them.
   a. Gog will fall upon the mountains of Israel and the beasts and birds will devour them (39:4-5).
   b. The Lord will send a fire on Gog and those in the isles, and they will know that Jehovah is the Lord. His name will not be polluted anymore (39:6–7).
4. Ezekiel 39:8–16. The day the Lord has spoken of has come. His holy name is known among his people Israel, and he will not allow them to pollute his name anymore. The heathen

shall know Jehovah is the Lord.

    a. The weapons will be burned by Israel instead of the wood of the forest (39:9–10).

    b. Gog will be given graves in Israel that smell and will be called Hamon-gog (39:11).

    c. Israel will bury Gog "and all his multitude" for seven months and search for others until the land is cleansed (39:12–16).

5. Ezekiel 39:17–24. The fowls and beasts of the field are invited to gather for the great sacrifice of flesh and blood.

    a. They will be filled with horses and mighty men (39:18–20).

    b. The heathen will see the judgment of the Lord (39:21).

    c. The house of Israel will know Jehovah is God from that day forward (39:22).

    d. The heathen will know that the people "of Israel went into captivity for their iniquity" (39:23–24).

6. Ezekiel 39:25–29. The Lord will have mercy on the whole house of Israel.

    a. Mercy will come after all those in the house of Israel have borne their shame for their trespasses (39:26).

    b. Mercy will come when Israel is gathered and the Lord is sanctified in the sight of many nations (39:27).

    c. Israel will know the Lord caused her to be led into captivity and gathered again (39:28).

    d. The Lord will not hide his face anymore; his spirit is poured out (39:29).

Notes and Commentary

The quote used in the beginning of this chapter is the only comment made by the Prophet Joseph Smith regarding Gog and Magog and probably does not refer to Ezekiel 38 and 39, nor did he make any changes in these chapters in his translations of the Bible. Rarely have these chapters been quoted by general authorities. The Lord revealed to the Prophet: "And the great and abominable church, which is the whore of all the earth, shall be cast down by devouring fire, according as it is spoken by the mouth of Ezekiel the prophet, who spoke of these things, which have not come to pass but surely must, as I live, for abominations shall not reign" (D&C 29:21). These events would have included these chapters. Cross references to biblical prophets also give assistance.

Elder McConkie has written more on these chapters than any other general authority. Parley P. Pratt and Joseph Fielding Smith are two others who have made some comments on these chapters. In addition, no Latter-day Saint scholars treat these chapters of Ezekiel very thoroughly. Noted Old Testament scholar Sidney B. Sperry only wrote one and a half pages on them.[2] Ellis Rasmussen, another Old Testament scholar, has also allotted only one and a half pages for these chapters.[3] Commentaries by those of other faiths are of little help either; therefore, these chapters are applicable to Joseph Smith's statement as he was discussing the Book of Daniel: "I make this broad declaration, that whenever God gives a vision of an image, or beast, or figure of any kind, He always holds Himself responsible to give a revelation or interpretation of the meaning thereof, otherwise we are not responsible or accountable for our belief in it. Don't be afraid of being damned for not knowing the meaning of a vision or figure, if God has not given a revelation or interpretation of the subject."[4] Consequently, the approach to these chapters will rely heavily on Elder Bruce R. McConkie with periodic comments of others interspersed. The text will often be broken down to a single verse or two to make the comments easier to follow.

A prophecy against Gog
(Ezekiel 38:1–2)

And the word of the Lord came unto me, saying, Son of man, set thy face against Gog, the land of Magog, the chief prince of Meshech and Tubal, and prophesy.

Elder McConkie explained:

Ezekiel gives us another view and perspective of what shall be when the armies from the north invade the glorious land. This is the religious war of which Daniel spoke. It is a holy war in which emotion rules and ways of worship are at stake. It is a war between Christ and his gospel, and Lucifer who sought to deny men their agency even before the world was. In it we shall see Christ come to champion the cause of his people, and in it we shall see the fall of the great and abominable church, which is the church of the devil. She shall fall as Babylon of old fell.

Elder McConkie continues and explains that Gog and Magog are all the nations of the earth who take up the sword against Israel and Jerusalem in the day of Armageddon. Their identities remain to be revealed when the battle alliances are made.[5]

The Lord will turn Gog back
(Ezekiel 38:3-4)

And say, Thus saith the Lord God; Behold, I am against thee, O Gog, the chief prince of Meshech and Tubal: and I will turn thee back, and put hooks into thy jaws, and I will bring thee forth, and all thine army, horses and horsemen, all of them clothed with all sorts of armour, even a great company with bucklers and shields, all of them handling swords.

Elder McConkie wrote:

Ezekiel's prophetic utterances begin with the divine assurance that Gog and Magog and all their armies shall be defeated. It could not be otherwise. God and his purposes must and shall prevail. To all these nations, combined in one great and evil enterprise against his people, the Lord says: [quotes v. 4]. Their weaponry and military prowess and massive strength shall be of no moment in that day. The Lord himself is governing the outcome of the battle. Gog and all his multitudes shall fall and fail, and shall be as when God overthrew Sodom and Gomorrah.[6]

"Hooks into thy jaws" (39:4) reminds us of the Lord speaking of Assyria in Isaiah's day (Isaiah 37:29). The battle in the "valley of decision" (Joel 3:14) describes the same event as Ezekiel does above.

"I will also gather all nations, and will bring them down into the valley of Jehoshaphat, and will plead with them there for my people and for my heritage Israel, whom they have scattered among the nations, and parted my land: . . . Assemble yourselves, and come, all ye heathen, and gather yourselves together round about: thither cause thy mighty ones to come down, O Lord. Let the heathen be wakened, and come up to the valley of Jehoshaphat: for there will I sit to judge all the heathen round about" (Joel 3:2, 11–12).[7]

A warning to prepare
(Ezekiel 38:5-9)

Persia, Ethiopia, and Libya with them; all of them with shield and helmet: Gomer, and all his bands; the house of Togarmah of the north quarters, and all his bands: and many people with thee. Be thou prepared, and prepare for thyself, thou, and all thy company that are assembled unto thee, and be thou a guard unto them.

After many days thou shalt be visited: in the latter years thou shalt come into the land that is brought back from the sword, and is gathered out of many people, against the mountains of Israel, which have been always waste: but it is brought forth out of the nations, and they shall dwell safely all of them. Thou shalt ascend and come like a storm, thou shalt be like a cloud to cover the land, thou, and all thy bands, and many people with thee.

The names of these countries of Ezekiel's time are undoubtedly symbolic of the Gentile nations of the last days. Elder McConkie made the following comments on these verses:

The destined events are these: "In the latter years" [v. 8], Israel shall return to her land, coming out of all the nations of the earth. Old Jerusalem shall be rebuilt and the latter-day temple shall stand within its walls. When the appointed time comes to assemble all nations to fight against Jerusalem, Gog and Magog shall come according to this promise. "Thou shalt ascend and come like a storm, thou shalt be like a cloud to cover the land, thou, and all thy bands, and many people with thee" [v. 9].

Nations that go to war are engaged in either righteous or evil causes. The Lamanite assaults were evil; the Nephite defenses were righteous. Israel's attacks on the Amorites and other inhabitants of Canaan were directed by the Lord and were right. When the Philistines came against David and his people, their cause was evil. It was the will of the Lord that the American colonies free themselves from European domination in the Revolutionary War and so their cause was just. Armageddon will be a war of aggression instituted by Gog and Magog. Theirs will be an evil cause. Those nations that defend Israel and Jerusalem will be doing what the Lord wants. To them it will be a righteous war.[8]

Think an evil thought
(Ezekiel 38:10–11)

Thus saith the Lord God; It shall also come to pass, that at the same time shall things come into thy mind, and thou shalt think an evil thought: and thou shalt say, I will go up to the land of unwalled villages; I will go to them that are at rest, that dwell safely, all of them dwelling without walls, and having neither bars nor gates.

Concerning verse 10, Elder McConkie wrote: "Is not this also the case with all nations that seek to subjugate and enslave other peoples and nations."[9] Concerning verse 11, Elder McConkie wrote: "The Destructive power of their weapons will be so great that it will be as though the cities of the earth were unwalled villages."[10] Dr. Sydney B. Sperry commented: "The enemy thinks he will have an easy time of it plundering peaceful, unwalled villages (38:10–12), but though they (the enemy) come as a cloud, the Lord has different ideas."[11]

To the victor belong the spoils
(Ezekiel 38:12-13)

To take a spoil, and to take a prey; to turn thine hand upon the desolate places that are now inhabited, and upon the people that are gathered out of the nations, which have gotten cattle and goods, that dwell in the midst of the land. Sheba, and Dedan, and the merchants of Tarshish, with all the young lions thereof, shall say unto thee, Art thou come to take a spoil? hast thou gathered thy company to take a prey? to carry away silver and gold, to take away cattle and goods, to take a great spoil?

Regarding verse 12, Elder McConkie said, "Conquerors steal from their victims. Nebuchadnezzar takes the golden vessels from the temple. Hitler makes bare the art galleries of France. Gog and Magog shall confiscate the wealth of Israel, and those who see it shall say [quotes from Ezekiel 38:13]."[12]

Elder McConkie commented on verse 13, "To the victor belong the spoils; the mere fact that Armageddon is a religious war will not deny Gog his gold."[13]

Gog in the latter days
(Ezekiel 38:14-16)

Therefore, son of man, prophesy and say unto Gog, Thus saith the Lord God; In that day when my people of Israel dwelleth safely, shalt thou not know it?

And thou shalt come from thy place out of the north parts, thou, and many people with thee, all of them riding upon horses, a great company, and a mighty army:

And thou shalt come up against my people of Israel, as a cloud to cover the land; it shall be in the latter days, and I will bring thee against my land, that the heathen may know me, when I shall be sanctified in thee, O Gog, before their eyes.

Elder McConkie exclaimed: "O Gog, O Magog, how great are thy hosts; how strong is thy armor; how destructive is thy power! When thou falleth, with all thy greatness, all men will know that God alone could defeat such dread and fearsome hosts."[14]

Great shaking in the land of Israel
(Ezekiel 38:17□20)

Thus saith the Lord God; Art thou he of whom I have spoken in old time by my servants the prophets of Israel, which prophesied in those days many years that I would bring thee against them?

And it shall come to pass at the same time when Gog shall come against the land of Israel, saith the Lord God, that my fury shall come up in my face.

For in my jealousy and in the fire of my wrath have I spoken, Surely in that day there shall be a great shaking in the land of Israel;

So that the fishes of the sea, and the fowls of the heaven, and the beasts of the field, and all creeping things that creep upon the earth, and all the men that are upon the face of the earth, shall shake at my presence, and the mountains shall be thrown down, and the steep places shall fall, and every wall shall fall to the ground.

Elder McConkie wrote:

We suppose all of the prophets in Israel spoke more or less about the second coming of the King of Israel and about the wars and desolations that would precede and attend that dreadful day. The preserved words of many of them testify of that which is to be in the last days. Isaiah tells us of the fire and blood and desolation that will attend the Second Coming, and that "the slain of the Lord shall be many" in that day (Isaiah 66:16). Jeremiah says the Lord will "call for a sword upon all the inhabitants of the earth. . . . And the slain of the Lord shall be at that day from one end of the earth even unto the other end of the earth" (Jeremiah 25:29, 33). Zechariah sets forth in extensor what shall take place when the Lord gathers "all nations against Jerusalem" (Zechariah 12–14). Zephaniah devotes almost the entire three chapters of his writings to the same thing. So also does Joel. Daniel and Malachi in due course will open their mouths on the same matters. There is nothing hidden or secret about the general course of events that the Lord God shall bring to pass in his own good time, a time that is now not far distant.[15]

Elder Parley P. Pratt wrote:

> Oh! Ye blind, ye stiff-necked, ye hard-hearted generation, with the Bible circulated among all nations, will whole nations be so blind as to fulfill this prophecy, and not know it until it brings destruction upon their own heads? Why all this blindness? Alas! it is because of false teachers, who will tell them the Bible must be spiritualized. Others declare that these prophecies can never be understood until they are fulfilled. If this be the case, then we can never escape the judgments predicted in them, but must continue the children of darkness, until they come upon us unawares and sweep us from the earth. Then where will be the consolation in looking back and seeing them fulfilled?[16]

Many, many passages speak of the Lord's anger (i.e., those who "do evil in the sight of the Lord thy God, to provoke him to anger;" Deuteronomy 4:25). The coming of Gog against the land of Israel will provoke God to anger.

Elder McConkie made this analogy of verses 18–19: "This is the mighty earthquake when the Mount of Olives cleaves and mountains and valleys and continents change their shapes."[17]

Elder McConkie gave this interpretation of verse 20: "This refers to the moment of the Lord's return. All things shall shake at his presence. The earthquakes and the trembling and the distortions of the landmasses of our planet shall take place when he comes to dwell again among men."[18] President Joseph Fielding Smith adds that "there are many prophecies in the Bible bearing the restoration of continents and islands again."[19]

Every man's sword against his brother
(Ezekiel 38:21-23)

And I will call for a sword against him throughout all my mountains, saith the Lord God: every man's sword shall be against his brother. And I will plead against him with pestilence and with blood; and I will rain upon him, and upon his bands, and upon the many people that are with him, an overflowing rain, and great hailstones, fire, and brimstone. Thus will I magnify myself, and sanctify myself; and I will be known in the eyes of many nations, and they shall know that I am the Lord.

These verses apply to "all [the Lord's] mountains" (38:21). Joseph Smith described the conditions in America, or the mountains of Zion, in the last days.

The time is soon coming, when no man will have any peace but in Zion and her stakes. I saw men hunting the lives of their own sons, and brother murdering brother, women killing their own daughters, and daughters seeking the lives of their mothers. I saw armies arrayed against armies. I saw blood, desolation, fires. The Son of Man has said that the mother shall be against the daughter, and the daughter against the mother. These things are at our doors. They will follow the Saints of God from city to city. Satan will rage, and the spirit of the devil is now enraged. I know not how soon these things will take place; but with a view of them, shall I cry peace? No; I will lift up my voice and testify of them. How long you will have good crops, and the famine be kept off, I do not know; when the fig tree leaves, know then that the summer is nigh at hand.[20]

Elder McConkie applied these same verses to Jerusalem and then extended them to all the world: "What of Gog and all his hosts in that dread day? What of the nations who have come to battle against the chosen people? Ezekiel's accounts are not chronological, and much that he recites will require periods of time to accomplish. But incident to the Second Coming, this word will be fulfilled [quotes verse 21].

This, in truth, will be a worldwide conflict; the sword that is wielded in the mountains of Israel will be the same sword that slays men in all nations [quotes verse 22]."[21]

Elder McConkie then explains: "It shall be, in the literal and full sense of the word, as it was with Sodom and Gomorrah. Fire and brimstone will fall upon the armies of the wicked in all nations. That which is going forward in Palestine is but a type and a shadow of that which shall be in all nations and among all peoples. We must remind ourselves that this is a worldwide conflict and that all nations are involved."[22]

Elder McConkie comments regarding verse 23: "All men will know that no power save the power of God can bring to pass that which has thus been brought to pass."[23]

Prophecies against Gog
(Ezekiel 39:1-3)

Therefore, thou son of man, prophesy against Gog, and say, Thus saith the Lord God; Behold, I am against thee, O Gog, the chief prince of Meshech and Tubal: and I will turn thee back, and leave but the sixth part of thee, and will cause thee to come up from the north parts, and will bring thee upon the mountains of Israel: and I will smite thy bow out of thy left hand, and will cause thine arrows to fall out of thy right hand.

As outlined in the beginning of the chapter, Ezekiel 38 describes the coming of Gog against Jerusalem. In chapter 39, Ezekiel prophesies against Gog. Elder McConkie quotes the first verses of chapter 39 with the following comments:

We now come to the prophetic word about the destruction of Gog and Magog, and all the nations that have forsaken the Lord, and all the wicked in all the earth. "I am against thee, O Gog," saith the Lord. "And I will turn thee back, and leave but the sixth part of thee." Gog, who came from the "north parts" to do battle "upon the mountains of Israel", shall return to the lands whence she came. But she will leave five dead bodies behind for every one live man who returns. She came, a mighty host, like a storm and like a cloud covering the land; she shall return, few in number, bowed and beaten by the rains of the Almighty.[24]

Elder McConkie declares: "Her weapons of war will not serve their purpose; she will be without oil for her war machines, and her bullets will be defective and not find their marks."[25]

Gog upon the mountains of Israel
(Ezekiel 39:4-5)

Thou shalt fall upon the mountains of Israel, thou, and all thy bands, and the people that is with thee: I will give thee unto the ravenous birds of every sort, and to the beasts of the field to be devoured. Thou shalt fall upon the open field: for I have spoken it, saith the Lord God.

Elder McConkie wrote, "Death and destruction shall leave the slain of the Lord in all the earth. . . . Pestilence, plagues, disease shall sweep as a desolating scourge through the ranks of the armed ones. And the weapons of war in the hands of the defenders of Israel shall take their toll. Dead bodies, unburied, will litter the land.[26]

The Lord will send fire on Gog
(Ezekiel 39:6-10)

And I will send a fire on Magog, and among them that dwell carelessly in the isles: and they shall know that I am the Lord. So will I make my holy name known in the midst of my people Israel; and I will not let them pollute my holy name any more: and the heathen shall know that I am the Lord, the Holy One in Israel.

Behold, it is come, and it is done, saith the Lord God; this is the day whereof I have spoken. And they that dwell in the cities of Israel shall go forth, and shall set on fire and burn the weapons, both the shields and the bucklers, the bows, and the arrows, and the handstaves, and the spears, and they shall burn them with fire seven years:

So that they shall take no wood out of the field, neither cut down any out of the forests; for they shall burn the weapons with fire: and they shall spoil those that spoiled them, and rob those that robbed them, saith the Lord God.

Elder McConkie declares, "None but the Lord himself can cause the elements to melt with fervent heat so that every corruptible thing is consumed. . . . How could it be otherwise? The wicked are destroyed, and the heathen nations—yet to hear the gospel and be converted—

shall have all these great wondrous signs before them."[27]

Elder McConkie continues: "This is the day! Oh, blessed day! The Lord reigns; the year of his redeemed has come; this is the day! At this point in his prophetic utterances—which are not and were not intended to be chronological—Ezekiel tells in graphic language of the aftermath of the defeat of Gog and Magog by the sword. We would be derelict if we did not quote his very words, words written by the power of the Spirit. They are indeed the words of the Lord himself."[28]

Elder McConkie continues: "It seems to us as we consider this coming eventuality that almost all of the wealth of the world will have been spent for weapons of war. It is indeed Lucifer's last chance to destroy the souls of men on the field of battle before he is bound and has no power for the space of a thousand years. From the standpoint of time all this must take place before the cleansing fires prepare the earth for the abode of the Clean One."[29]

Seven months burying Gog's dead
(Ezekiel 39:11–12)

And it shall come to pass in that day, that I will give unto Gog a place there of graves in Israel, the valley of the passengers on the east of the sea: and it shall stop the noses of the passengers: and there shall they bury Gog and all his multitude: and they shall call it The valley of Hamon-gog. And seven months shall the house of Israel be burying of them, that they may cleanse the land.

Elder McConkie observed: "Has there ever been such an enterprise as this? Will there ever be such a graveyard as Palestine? There the embalmed bodies of the righteous rest in sacred tombs, awaiting the sound of the trump of God that shall call them forth in the resurrection of life; and there the mangled carcasses of the wicked shall lie in unmarked graves, awaiting the sound of a later trump that will call them forth in the resurrection of damnation."[30]

The face of the earth cleansed
(Ezekiel 39:13–16)

Yea, all the people of the land shall bury them; and it shall be to them a renown the day that I shall be glorified, saith the Lord God. And they shall sever out men of continual employment, passing through the land to bury with the passengers those that remain upon the face of the earth, to cleanse it: after the end of seven months shall they search. And the passengers that pass through the land, when any seeth a man's bone, then shall he set up a sign by it, till the buriers have buried it in the valley of Hamon-gog. And also the name of the city shall be Hamonah. Thus shall they cleanse the land.

Elder McConkie concluded:

As we close this portion of our analysis, we must note that the great war involving Gog and Magog is both premillennial, as we have here set forth, and also postmillennial in the sense that there will be another great conflict with wicked nations just before this globe becomes a celestial sphere. We shall speak of this hereafter. The similarities between the two great conflicts justify calling them by the same name. This John does in these words: "And when the thousand years are expired, Satan shall be loosed out of his prison, And shall go out to deceive the nations which are in the four quarters of the earth, Gog and Magog, to gather them together to battle: the number of whom is as the sand of the sea. And they went up on the breadth of the earth, and compassed the camp of the saints about, and the beloved city: and fire came down from God out of heaven, and devoured them" (Revelation 20:7–9).

As with some Messianic prophecies that speak of both the first and the second advents of our Lord in the same language, it may be that portions of Ezekiel's great prophecy are subject to dual fulfillment. Our concern is with what lies ahead for us. Postmillennial events will be revealed in full to those who live during the Millennium. The knowledge then given will stand as a warning for those of future generations, even as the words of Ezekiel warn us to live as becometh saints. We speculate that much the same thing that happens in the first war with Gog and Magog will be repeated in the second.[31]

Fowls and beasts will gorge themselves on the dead (Ezekiel 39:17-22)

And, thou son of man, thus saith the Lord God; Speak unto every feathered fowl, and to every beast of the field, Assemble yourselves, and come; gather yourselves on every side to my sacrifice that I do sacrifice for you, even a great sacrifice upon the mountains of Israel, that ye may eat flesh, and drink blood. Ye shall eat the flesh of the mighty, and drink the blood of the princes of the earth, of rams, of lambs, and of goats, of bullocks, all of them fatlings of Bashan. And ye shall eat fat till ye be full, and drink blood till ye be drunken, of my sacrifice which I have sacrificed for you. Thus ye shall be filled at my table with horses and chariots, with mighty men, and with all men of war, saith the Lord God. And I will set my glory among the heathen, and all the heathen shall see my judgment that I have executed, and my hand that I have laid upon them. So the house of Israel shall know that I am the Lord their God from that day and forward.

Elder McConkie wrote concerning verses 17–19:

> After the defeat by the sword of the armies of Gog and Magog, and in the day when the slain of the Lord cover the earth and are as dung upon its face, then the fowls and the beasts shall gorge themselves upon the flesh and blood of the dead. This awful happening, attended by all the stench and stink of the rotting corpses, is set forth in both the Old Testament and the New and in latter-day revelation. It will indeed be something to behold.
>
> The mountains of Israel are but the illustration; the same event will occur in all nations and among all peoples, for Armageddon knows no bounds.[32]

After quoting Ezekiel 39:18, Elder McConkie stated: "In that day the flesh and blood of the great and mighty of the earth shall be of no more worth than that of the animals of the fields."[33] He then quoted 39:19 and observed: "There neither has been nor will be any feast like unto this feast. What a blessing it will be for the earth to burn and be cleansed of its corruption and its filth."[34]

Elder McConkie compared Ezekiel's account with the vision of John the Revelator:

> John, in his visions of what was to be in the last days, saw "an angel standing in the sun" and heard him cry "to all the fowls that fly in the midst of heaven, Come and gather yourselves together unto the supper of the great God; That ye may eat the flesh of kings, and flesh of captains, and the flesh of mighty men, and the flesh of horses, and of them that sit on them, and the flesh of all men, both free and bond, both small

and great" (Revelation 19:17–18). And our latter-day revelation, speaking of those who have fallen by the plagues and by the sword in Armageddon, says: "And it shall come to pass that the beasts of the forest and the fowls of the air shall devour them up" (D&C 29:20).

We have set forth, thus, what the inspired writers say about the blood-soaked scene of gore and corruption that is yet to be. It makes us wonder why it has been revealed in such detail in at least three dispensations. Certainly it will be a literal event in the coming day. But more than this, it surely bears witness of other truths that men should know. It testifies that wickedness shall cover the earth in the last days; that all nations shall take up the sword in the final war of the ages; that men in uncounted numbers will die of plagues and pestilence and by the edge of the sword; and that the dead bodies of all, kings and rulers included, heaped as dung upon the ground, shall, in death, have no more worth than the carcasses of the beasts of the field. Perhaps, above all else, the horror of it all stands as a call to wayward men to repent, to cease their warfare against God, and to seek an inheritance with his people, many of whom will be preserved in that dread day.[35]

Elder McConkie then analyzed the things that will grow out of the battle of Armageddon.[36] Another description of the Second Coming was given to the Prophet Joseph Smith by revelation in the Doctrine and Covenants.

But, behold, I say unto you that before this great day shall come the sun shall be darkened, and the moon shall be turned into blood, and the stars shall fall from heaven, and there shall be greater signs in heaven above and in the earth beneath;

And there shall be weeping and wailing among the hosts of men; and there shall be a great hailstorm sent forth to destroy the crops of the earth.

And it shall come to pass, because of the wickedness of the world, that I will take vengeance upon the wicked, for they will not repent; for the cup of mine indignation is full; for behold, my blood shall not cleanse them if they hear me not. 18.

Wherefore, I the Lord God will send forth flies upon the face of the earth, which shall take hold of the inhabitants thereof, and shall eat their flesh, and shall cause maggots to come in upon them;

And their tongues shall be stayed that they shall not utter against me; and their flesh shall fall from off their bones, and their eyes from their sockets;

And it shall come to pass that the beasts of the forest and the fowls of the air shall devour them up.

And the great and abominable church, which is the whore of all the earth, shall be cast down by devouring fire, according as it is spoken by the mouth of Ezekiel the prophet, who spoke of these things, which have not come to pass but surely must, as I live, for abominations shall not reign. (D&C 29:14–21)

Regarding the fall of the great and abominable church (D&C 29:21), Elder McConkie concluded:

Now, Ezekiel spoke only of devouring fire—of fire and brimstone—being rained upon Gog and Magog and all the nations that fought against Israel. He made no mention of a great and abominable church being involved, but the Lord here tells us that it was, in fact, the great whore of all the earth who was being destroyed by the fire. That is to say, there is both a political and an ecclesiastical kingdom of Lucifer on earth. It is with his kingdom as it is with the Lord's. There is an ecclesiastical kingdom of God on earth that is The Church of Jesus Christ of Latter-day Saints, and there shall be a political kingdom of God on earth in that day when the kingdom is restored to Israel and the Lord himself reigns. Satan's kingdom is composed of all that is evil and corrupt and carnal and wicked no matter where it is found. He operates through what we call churches, and he operates through what we call governments. Both are part of his kingdom. And in the final great day that lies ahead, the fall of one will be the fall of the other. When Babylon falls, she will take with her the churches of the world and the nations of the world. As the Lord makes a full end of all nations, so he will make a full end of all evil churches. Men will be free to believe as they choose during the Millennium, but the great and abominable church, the whore of all the earth, will no longer be among men, because the wicked portion of mankind will have been burned as stubble.

At Armageddon that great political power which "seeketh to overthrow the freedom of all lands, nations, and countries," and which "bringeth to pass the destruction of all people," and which is itself "built up by the devil" (Ether 8:25)—that very political kingdom, in all its parts, shall be burned with fire. It is the great and abominable church.

And thus out of Armageddon and the burning of the vineyard will come the great millennial blessings for all those who abide the day, the great and dreadful day of the Lord.[37]

There are several other references in the Doctrine and Covenants that declare the (spiritual) fall of Babylon (see D&C 1:16; 35:11; 64:24; 133:7, 14).

Mercy upon the whole house of Israel (Ezekiel 39:23-29)

And the heathen shall know that the house of Israel went into captivity for their iniquity: because they trespassed against me, therefore hid I my face from them, and gave them into the hand of their enemies: so fell they all by the sword. According to their uncleanness and according to their transgressions have I done unto them, and hid my face from them. Therefore thus saith the Lord God; Now will I bring again the captivity of Jacob, and have mercy upon the whole house of Israel, and will be jealous for my holy name; after that they have borne their shame, and all their trespasses whereby they have trespassed against me, when they dwelt safely in their land, and none made them afraid. When I have brought them again from the people, and gathered them out of their enemies' lands, and am sanctified in them in the sight of many nations; then shall they know that I am the Lord their God, which caused them to be led into captivity among the heathen: but I have gathered them unto their own land, and have left none of them any more there. Neither will I hide my face any more from them: for I have poured out my spirit upon the house of Israel, saith the Lord God.

The heathen shall know why Israel was taken into captivity. They shall also have their opportunity to hear the gospel. The Lord confirmed this message from Ezekiel with a revelation to Joseph Smith:

That through your administration they may receive the word, and through their administration the word may go forth unto the ends of the earth, unto the Gentiles first, and then, behold, and lo, they shall turn unto the Jews.

And then cometh the day when the arm of the Lord shall be revealed in power in convincing the nations, the heathen nations, the house of Joseph, of the gospel of their salvation.

For it shall come to pass in that day, that every man shall hear the fulness of the gospel in his own tongue, and in his own language, through those who are ordained unto this power, by the administration of the Comforter, shed forth upon them for the revelation of Jesus Christ. (D&C 90:9–11)

They are probably linked with the house of Joseph because Joseph holds the birthright, and the heathen converts will be adopted into the tribe of Joseph. "The heathen" (Ezekiel 39:23) refer to the non-Christian nations. The Gentiles are the Christian nations (see 3 Nephi 16:6).

As the Lord said, the opportunity for the heathen nations to hear the gospel will be after the house of Israel is gathered. Ezekiel concludes these two chapters with the Lord's promise to bring Israel out of captivity among the nations of the earth (39:28).

Summary of Chapters 38–39

The great battle of Gog and Magog, or more specifically Armageddon, is described more fully by Ezekiel than any other Bible prophet. Thanks to Elder McConkie's commentary on the text of Ezekiel, we are further enlightened concerning this last great battle. We must study the scriptures and the words of modern day prophets and constantly prepare ourselves to be a part of the Lord's army by preaching the gospel and following the counsel of the Lord's prophet. By doing so, we may avoid, as far as possible, the effects of this terrible war.

Notes

1. Joseph Smith, *Teachings of the Prophet Joseph Smith,* sel. Joseph Fielding Smith (Salt Lake City: Deseret Book, 1976), 280.
2. Sidney B. Sperry, *The Voice of Israel's Prophets* (Salt Lake City: Deseret Book, 1952), 228–29.
3. Ellis Rasmussen, *A Latter-day Saint Commentary on the Old Testament* (Salt Lake City: Deseret Book, 1993), 609–10.
4. Smith, *Teachings,* 291.
5. Bruce R. McConkie, *The Millennial Messiah* (Salt Lake City: Deseret Book, 1982), 481.
6. Ibid.

7. For a more detailed commentary on Joel 3, see Monte S. Nyman and Farres H. Nyman, *The Words of the Twelve Prophets* (Salt Lake City: Deseret Book, 1990), 43–46.

8. McConkie, *The Millennial Messiah*, 481–82.

9. Ibid., 482.

10. Ibid.

11. Sperry, *Voice of Israel's Prophets*, 229.

12. McConkie, *The Millennial Messiah*, 482–83.

13. Ibid., 483.

14. Ibid.

15. Ibid., 483–84.

16. Parley P. Pratt, *Key to the Science of Theology* (Salt Lake City: Deseret Book, 1978), 32.

17. McConkie, *The Millennial Messiah*, 484.

18. Ibid.

19. Joseph Fielding Smith, *Answers to Gospel Questions*, 5 vols. (Salt Lake City: Deseret Book, 1963), 4:21–24. President Smith also quotes Isaiah 54: 9–10, Revelation 16–20, and D&C 133:21–24; see also Joseph Fielding Smith, *The Signs of the Times* (Salt Lake City: Deseret Book, 1970), 46–48.

20. Smith, *Teachings*, 161.

21. McConkie, *The Millennial Messiah*, 484–85.

22. Ibid., 485.

23. Ibid.

24. Ibid.

25. Ibid.

26. Ibid., 486.

27. Ibid.

28. Ibid.

29. Ibid., 487.

30. Ibid., 488.

31. Ibid.

32. Ibid., 488–89.

33. Ibid., 489.

34. Ibid.

35. Ibid., 489–90.

36. The reader is encouraged to read pages 490–94 in *The Millennial Messiah*.

37. McConkie, *The Millennial Messiah*, 493–94.

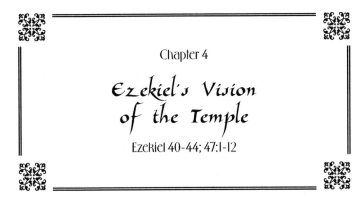

Chapter 4

Ezekiel's Vision of the Temple

Ezekiel 40-44; 47:1-12

he Prophet Joseph Smith taught that the main object of the gathering of the Jews, or the people of God in any age of the world, was to build a temple.

The main object was to build unto the Lord a house whereby He could reveal unto His people the ordinances of His house and the glories of His kingdom, and teach the people the way of salvation; for there are certain ordinances and principles that, when they are taught and practiced, must be done in a place or house built for that purpose.

It was the design of the councils of heaven before the world was, that the principles and laws of the priesthood should be predicated upon the gathering of the people in every age of the world. Jesus did everything to gather the people, and they would not be gathered, and He therefore poured out curses upon them. Ordinances instituted in the heavens before the foundation of the world, in the priesthood, for the salvation of men, are not to be altered or changed. All must be saved on the same principles.

It is for the same purpose that God gathers together His people in the last days, to build unto the Lord a house to prepare them for the ordinances and endowments, washings and anointings, etc.[1]

Ezekiel's vision of the temple has four different interpretations among Bible scholars. The first is a literal interpretation that a temple was to be built after the Jews returned from the seventy-year exile into Babylon. The second interpretation is that the vision is a symbolic representation of the Christian church. A third interpretation is that Ezekiel is seeing the latter-day temple that will be built for the millennial reign of Christ. The problem some see in this interpretation is that the festivals, sacrificies, priesthood, and Old Testament worship of the law of Moses would be reintroduced after the New Testament fulfillment of the law of Moses through Jesus Christ. The fourth interpretation is that these chapters are apocalyptic writing and must be interpreted as such, combining symbolism and the future.[2]

In my opinion, the interpretation of Ezekiel's vision is a combination of numbers three and four above. The temple is definitely a latter-day temple to be built in Jerusalem before the Second Coming. The description of temple worship under the law of Moses refers to the reintroduction of the law of Moses, as all things are gathered together in the dispensation of the fulness of times (see Ephesians 1:9–10), and is also symbolic of the fuller practice of the higher law of Christ.

The Prophet taught that the ordinances of sacrifice will again be practiced as part of the Restoration:

> It will be necessary here to make a few observations on the doctrine set forth in the above quotation, and it is generally supposed that sacrifice was entirely done away when the Great Sacrifice [i.e.,] the sacrifice of the Lord Jesus was offered up, and that there will be no necessity for the ordinance of sacrifice in future; but those who assert this are certainly not acquainted with the duties, privileges and authority of the Priesthood, or with the Prophets.
>
> The offering of sacrifice has ever been connected and forms a part of the duties of the Priesthood. It began with the Priesthood, and will be continued until after the coming of Christ, from generation to generation. We frequently have mention made of the offering of sacrifice by the servants of the Most High in ancient days, prior to the law of Moses; which ordinances will be continued when the Priesthood is restored with

all its authority, power and blessings....

These sacrifices, as well as every ordinance belonging to the Priesthood, will, when the Temple of the Lord shall be built, and the sons of Levi be purified, be fully restored and attended to in all their powers, ramifications, and blessings. This ever did and ever will exist when the powers of the Melchizedek Priesthood are sufficiently manifest; else how can the restitution of all things spoken of by the Holy Prophets be brought to pass. It is not to be understood that the law of Moses will be established again with all its rites and variety of ceremonies; this has never been spoken of by the prophets; but those things which existed prior to Moses' day, namely, sacrifice, will be continued.

It may be asked by some, what necessity for sacrifice, since the Great Sacrifice was offered? In answer to which, if repentance, baptism, and faith existed prior to the days of Christ, what necessity for them since that time? The Priesthood has descended in a regular line from father to son, through their succeeding generations.[3]

In describing Ezekiel's temple, Elder Bruce R. McConkie gives support for both literal and figurative sacrifices:

Worldly scholars, not knowing the purposes of the Lord where his people are concerned; not understanding the doctrine of the gathering of Israel in the last days; not being aware that the gospel was to be restored in the latter days; not knowing that temples are essential to the salvation of men no matter what age they live in—worldly scholars have assumed that Ezekiel's temple was not and will not be built. The truth is that its construction lies ahead. No doubt some of the recitations relative to it are figurative, though it is clear that some sacrificial ordinances are yet to be performed.[4]

The outline below will follow Ezekiel's terminology. The symbolism, as far as can be safely interpreted, will be discussed in the notes and commentary. The specific temple measurements seem irrelevant at this time; thus, many verses will be skipped over.

1. Ezekiel 40:1–49. In the twenty-fifth year of the captivity in Babylon, Ezekiel is carried into a very high mountain in the land of Israel and is shown in vision a man with a measuring reed to measure the building.

    a. He sees the gate looking to the east and the measurements for the gate, the chambers, the porch, the posts, and the windows (40:6–16).

    b. He sees the outward gate toward the north and the measurements of the gates, the chambers, and the windows (40:17–23).

    c. He sees the same things for the south gate (40:24–31).

    d. He sees the inner court toward the east and the north gate and chambers where the burnt offerings were washed and the sacrifices slain (40:32–43).

    e. He sees the chambers of the priests, the keepers of the house; the priests of Zadok, the sons of Levi; and the porch and its measurements (40:44–49).

2. Ezekiel 41–42. Ezekiel sees the temple with its measurements.

    a. He is shown the most holy place, the side chambers, and other measurements of the house (41–42).

    b. He is shown the table that is before the Lord (41:22).

    c. He sees the holy chambers where the priests will eat the most holy things and where they change their garments (42:13–14).

3. Ezekiel 43:1–27. Ezekiel is shown the glory of the Lord coming into the house by way of the gate that faced east.

    a. The Lord tells Ezekiel this is the place where he dwells, and if the people of Israel put away their whoredoms, he will dwell in their midst forever (43:7–9).

    b. Ezekiel is to show the people of Israel the form of the house, the ordinances, and all the laws, and write it in their sight that they may be ashamed of their iniquities. The whole top of the mountain will be most holy. The measurements are given (43:10–17).

    c. Ezekiel is told the ordinances of the altar that the priests of Levi are to make, and that the ordinances are to be performed for eight days in order for the Lord to accept the house (43:18–27).

4. Ezekiel 44–45. Ezekiel again beholds the glory of the Lord in

His house and is told the requirements for using the house.

    a. The gate toward the east of the outward sanctuary is shut and will not be opened. It is for the Lord (44:1–3).

    b. Strangers, uncircumcised of heart, and flesh will not come into the house. The Levites who went astray will be accountable, but they will be keepers of the house (44:4–14).

    c. The priests who kept the charge of the Lord's sanctuary will minister for Him clothed in the linen garments. They are not to defile themselves (44:15–31).

5. Ezekiel 47:1–12. Ezekiel is shown water coming out from under the temple.

    a. The waters issue toward the east and go into the sea; the waters will be healed (47:6–8).

    b. There will be a great multitude of fish and fishers, the miry places will be salty (47:9–11).

    c. On the bank of the river, trees will grow for meat and for medicine (47:12).

Notes and Commentary

General authorities have made few comments on these chapters, especially those that need some interpretation. Their comments are usually applications to the members' lives. The Prophet Joseph Smith does give us a few verifications for interpretation. The instructions for the building and use of temples built in the last days, as revealed in the Doctrine and Covenants, also shed further light on the building and use of the future temple in Jerusalem. The following comments should be helpful.

The Date of the revelation
(Ezekiel 40:1)

In the five and twentieth year of our captivity, in the beginning of the year, in the tenth day of the month, in the fourteenth year after that the city was smitten, in the selfsame day the hand of the Lord was upon me, and brought me thither.

The date of this revelation, the twenty-fifth year, first month, and tenth day of their captivity, is twenty years after Ezekiel was called to be a prophet. He was called in the fifth year of captivity (Ezekiel 1:2–3). This revelation was also given thirteen years after the other revelations (see Ezekiel 32), except for the one given two years after this revelation concerning the king of Babylon coming against Egypt (29:17–21). The other date mentioned in this verse, "the fourteenth year after the city was smitten," has reference to the Babylonian invasion. King Nebuchadnezzar invaded Jerusalem in the ninth year, tenth month, tenth day of the month (24:1–2). The invasion lasted two years; thus, it was the fourteenth year after the city fell.

Ezekiel is given a vision
(Ezekiel 40:2–4)

In the visions of God brought he me into the land of Israel, and set me upon a very high mountain, by which was as the frame of a city on the south.

And he brought me thither, and, behold, there was a man, whose appearance was like the appearance of brass, with a line of flax in his hand, and a measuring reed; and he stood in the gate.

And the man said unto me, Son of man, behold with thine eyes, and hear with thine ears, and set thine heart upon all that I shall shew thee; for to the intent that I might shew them unto thee art thou brought hither: declare all that thou seest to the house of Israel.

Ezekiel's being caught up into a very high mountain, where he was shown the future city of Jerusalem, is consistent with the Lord's pattern. Enoch was taken upon Mount Simeon where the heavens were opened to him (see Moses 7:2–3). Moses was caught up into "an exceeding high mountain" where he saw God and talked with him (Moses 1:1–2). Nephi was "caught away" into an exceedingly high mountain and shown the future of Jerusalem, the Nephites, and the Gentile nations (see 1 Nephi 11:1; Nephi 11–14). The Lord often uses mountains to communicate with his prophets when there is no temple.

The gate toward the east
(Ezekiel 40:6)

Then came he unto the gate which looketh toward the east, and went up the stairs thereof, and measured the threshold of the gate, which was the one reed broad; and the other threshold of the gate, which was one reed broad.

The gate toward the east may be the present-day "gate beautiful" or "golden gate" on the east side of the Jerusalem wall. Whether there will be any modification of this wall before the Savior comes is not known at this time. There will be no attempt to correlate the measurements given to Ezekiel of this gate or other parts of the wall with the present-day wall. Various Bibles and commentaries have attempted to sketch the holy mount and the temple, but these are possible measurements and not definite.

The chamber for the priests
(Ezekiel 40:44–46)

And without the inner gate were the chambers of the singers in the inner court, which was at the side of the north gate; and their prospect was toward the south: one at the side of the east gate having the prospect toward the north. And he said unto me, This chamber, whose prospect is toward the south, is for the priests, the keepers of the charge of the house. And the chamber whose prospect is toward the north is for the priests, the keepers of the charge of the altar: these are the sons of Zadok among the sons of Levi, which come near to the Lord to minister unto him.

The sons of Zadok among the sons of Levi were given responsibilities for ministering in the temple. More details of the assignment are given later (see comments on 44:15–16; 44:17–19).

The most holy place
(Ezekiel 41:1–4)

Afterward he brought me to the temple, and measured the posts, six cubits broad on the one side, and six cubits broad on the other side, which was the breadth of the tabernacle.

And the breadth of the door was ten cubits; and the sides of the door were five cubits on the one side, and five cubits on the other side: and he measured the length thereof, forty cubits: and the breadth, twenty cubits.

Then went he inward, and measured the post of the door, two cubits; and the door, six cubits; and the breadth of the door, seven cubits.

> So he measured the length thereof, twenty cubits; and the breadth twenty cubits, before the temple: and he said unto me, This is the most holy place.

The most holy place is also called "the Holiest of all" in the Book of Hebrews. Under the law of Moses, only the high priest could enter this part of the temple, and he went only once a year (Hebrews 9:1–7). Ezekiel does not say that he went in, but the angelic being giving him the tour did go in. Perhaps Ezekiel was inside because the angel speaks with him after measuring the holy place, which implies that they are both inside. However, most commentators assume Ezekiel did not enter. The function of "the most holy place" in New Testament times is not given. For some explanation of its purpose in latter-day temples, see the commentary concerning Ezekiel 44:1–3.

The table before the Lord
(Ezekiel 41:22)

> The altar of wood was three cubits high, and the length thereof two cubits; and the corners thereof, and the length thereof, and the walls thereof, were of wood: and he said unto me, This is the table that is before the Lord.

The "table that is before the Lord" was probably the same table shown to Moses on Mount Sinai on which were placed twelve loaves of shewbread (see Exodus 25:30; Leviticus 24:5–9). Again we wonder about the connection between the law of Moses and the latter days. The table was undoubtedly symbolic of procedures in latter-day temples; perhaps it was to be used in connection with records of the dead (see D&C 128:24).

The holy garment
(Ezekiel 42:13–14)

> Then said he unto me, The north chambers and the south chambers, which are before the separate place, they be holy chambers, where the priests that approach unto the Lord shall eat the most holy things: there shall they lay the most holy things, and the meat offering, and the sin offering, and the trespass offering; for the place is holy.
>
> When the priests enter therein, then shall they not go out of the holy place into the utter court, but there they shall lay their

garments wherein they minister; for they are holy; and shall put on other garments, and shall approach to those things which are for the people.

These verses discuss the wearing of special clothing to minister in the temple. There are other references to special clothing later in these chapters (see Ezekiel 44:17–19). The purpose of the clothing is not given but has symbolic purposes. Elder Boyd K. Packer has written, "As with the ceremonies and ordinances of the temple, outside of the temple we say very little about the clothing worn inside. We can say that it, like the ceremonies, has great symbolic meaning."[5]

The place the Lord dwells
(Ezekiel 43:2-9)

And, behold, the glory of the God of Israel came from the way of the east: and his voice was like a noise of many waters: and the earth shined with his glory. And it was according to the appearance of the vision which I saw, even according to the vision that I saw when I came to destroy the city: and the visions were like the vision that I saw by the river Chebar; and I fell upon my face. And the glory of the Lord came into the house by the way of the gate whose prospect is toward the east. So the spirit took me up, and brought me into the inner court; and behold, the glory of the Lord filled the house. And I heard him speaking unto me out of the house; and the man stood by me. And he said unto me, Son of man, the place of my throne, and the place of the soles of my feet, where I will dwell in the midst of the children of Israel for ever, and my holy name, shall the house of Israel no more defile, neither they, nor their kings, by their whoredom, nor by the carcases of their kings in their high places. In their setting of their threshold by my thresholds, and their post by my posts, and the wall between me and them, they have even defiled my holy name by their abominations that they have committed: wherefore I have consumed them in mine anger. Now let them put away their whoredom, and the carcases of their kings, far from me, and I will dwell in the midst of them for ever.

Concerning the glory of the Lord and his voice described in these verses, Elder McConkie has written:

Ezekiel saw in vision "the glory of the God of Israel," and "his voice was like a noise of many waters: and the earth shined with his glory." With reference to the Lord's holy sanctuary, the voice said: "Son of man, the place of my throne, and the place of the soles of my feet, where I will dwell in the midst of the children of Israel for ever, and my holy name, shall the house of Israel no more defile. . . . And I will dwell in the midst of them for ever" (Ezekiel 43:2–9). His throne shall be in his holy house; his reign shall be a personal one, even the very soles of his feet again treading the dust of the earth; and Israel shall honor and serve him.[6]

Elder McConkie also wrote concerning the throne in the temple mentioned in verse 7, "It is clear that Ezekiel's Temple, to be built by the Jews in Jerusalem, is destined for millennial use. In chapter 43, for instance, the Lord calls it, specifically, 'the place of my throne, and the place of the soles of my feet, where I will dwell in the midst of the children of Israel for ever.' That is to say, it will be the place of his throne during the Millennium when he dwells among the house of Israel."[7]

Elder Orson Pratt also spoke of the Lord's throne in the temple:

And when he descends with all his Saints on that mountain [Mount of Olives], and this great convulsion of the earth takes place, then will Jesus proceed down to the new gate that will be built on the east side of the temple—the east gate of the temple, and he will enter into that temple and will seat himself on the throne that will be built in that temple. Ezekiel when describing this, in the 43rd chapter of his prophecy, says, or rather the Lord through Ezekiel says, "Son of man behold the place of my throne, and the place of the soles of my feet where I will dwell in the midst of the children of Israel for ever. And they shall no more defile my name," and so forth [v. 7]. Here is a prediction that, in that temple will be a certain apartment dedicated and set apart for the throne of the Lord, where he will sit, as the Prophet Zachariah and many of the Apostles have predicted, on the throne of his father David, and judge the whole house of Israel. Dwell with them personally, be in their midst.[8]

"The glory of the Lord filled the house" refers to the Lord accepting his house (Ezekiel 43:5, 27). Ezekiel saw this future glorious occasion. The acceptance of the Kirtland temple in 1836 was such an experience. The Prophet Joseph Smith, in his dedicatory prayer given to him by revelation (see D&C 109 section heading), asked that the temple would be filled with glory (D&C 109:37). The Lord appeared and accepted the house (D&C 110:7). A description of this event is given in the *History of the Church*:

> Brother George A. Smith arose and began to prophesy, when a noise was heard like the sound of a rushing mighty wind, which filled the Temple, and all the congregation simultaneously arose, being moved upon by an invisible power; many began to speak in tongues and prophesy; others saw glorious visions; and I beheld the Temple was filled with angels, which fact I declared to the congregation. The people of the neighborhood came running together (hearing an unusual sound within, and seeing a bright light like a pillar of fire resting upon the Temple), and were astonished at what was taking place. This continued until the meeting closed at eleven P.M.[9]

The law of the house
(Ezekiel 43:10–12)

> Thou son of man, shew the house to the house of Israel, that they may be ashamed of their iniquities: and let them measure the pattern.
>
> And if they be ashamed of all that they have done, shew them the form of the house, and the fashion thereof, and the goings out thereof, and the comings in thereof, and all the forms thereof, and all the ordinances thereof, and all the forms thereof, and all the laws thereof: and write it in their sight, that they may keep the whole form thereof, and all the ordinances thereof, and do them.
>
> This is the law of the house; Upon the top of the mountain the whole limit thereof round about shall be most holy. Behold, this is the law of the house.

Elder James E. Talmage spoke of the temple shown to Ezekiel and then quoted Ezekiel 43:10–12 to show the purpose of the revelation.

> In most of its essential features Ezekiel's ideal followed closely the plan of Solomon's Temple; so close, indeed, is the resemblance, that many of the details specified by Ezekiel have been accepted as those of the splendid edifice destroyed by Nebuchadnezzar. A predominant characteristic of the Temple described by Ezekiel was the spaciousness of its premises and the

symmetry of both the Holy House and its associated buildings. The area was to be a square of five hundred cubits, walled about and provided with a gateway and arches on each of three sides; on the west side the wall was to be unbroken by arch or portal. At each of the gateways were little chambers regarded as lodges, and provided with porches. In the outer court were other chambers. The entire area was to be elevated, and a flight of steps led to each gateway. In the inner court was seen the great altar, standing before the House, and occupying the center of a square of one hundred cubits. Ample provision was made for every variety of sacrifice and offering, and for the accommodation of the priests, the singers, and all engaged in the holy ritual. The main structure comprised a Porch, a Holy Place, and an inner sanctuary or Most Holy Place, the last named elevated above the rest and reached by steps. The plan provided for even greater exclusiveness than had characterized the sacred area of the Temple of Solomon; the double courts contributed to this end. The service of the Temple was prescribed in detail; the ordinances of the altar, the duties of the priests, the ministry of the Levites, the regulations governing oblations and feasts were all set forth.

The immediate purpose of this revelation through the vision of the prophet appears to have been that of awakening the people of Israel to a realization of their fallen state and a conception of their departed glory.[10]

The ordinances of the altar
(Ezekiel 43:18-27)

And he said unto me, Son of man, thus saith the Lord God; These are the ordinances of the altar in the day when they shall make it, to offer burnt offerings thereon, and to sprinkle blood thereon.

And thou shalt give to the priests the Levites that be of the seed of Zadok, which approach unto me, to minister unto me, saith the Lord God, a young bullock for a sin offering.

And thou shalt take of the blood thereof, and put it on the four horns of it, and on the four corners of the settle, and upon the border round about: thus shalt thou cleanse and purge it.

Thou shalt take the bullock also of the sin offering, and he shall burn it in the appointed place of the house, without the sanctuary.

And on the second day thou shalt offer a kid of the goats without blemish for a sin offering; and they shall cleanse the altar, as they did cleanse it with the bullock.

When thou hast made an end of cleansing it, thou shalt offer a young bullock without blemish, and a ram out of the flock without blemish.

And thou shalt offer them before the Lord, and the priests shall cast salt upon them, and they shall offer them up for a burnt offering unto the Lord.

Seven days shalt thou prepare every day a goat for a sin offering: they shall also prepare a young bullock, and a ram out of the flock, without blemish.

Seven days shall they purge the altar and purify it; and they shall consecrate themselves.

And when these days are expired, it shall be, that upon the eighth day, and so forward, the priests shall make your burnt offerings upon the altar, and your peace offerings; and I will accept you, saith the Lord God.

The offering of the sons of Levi described in these verses has both a literal and symbolic meaning. The Prophet said regarding Malachi's prophecy that the sons of Levi would make an offering again in righteousness (see Malachi 3:3) "when the temple of the Lord shall be built, and the sons of Levi be purified, be fully restored and attended to in all their powers, ramifications and blessings."[11] In the symbolic sense, the Prophet declared:

Behold, the great day of the Lord is at hand; and who can abide the day of his coming, and who can stand when he appeareth? For he is like a refiner's fire, and like fuller's soap; and he shall sit as a refiner and purifier of silver, and he shall purify the sons of Levi, and purge them as gold and silver, that they may offer unto the Lord an offering in righteousness. Let us, therefore, as a church and a people, and as Latter-day Saints, offer unto the Lord an offering in righteousness; and let us present in his holy temple, when it is finished, a book containing the records of our dead, which shall be worthy of all acceptation (D&C 128:24).

President Joseph Fielding Smith commented on what type of offering will be made by the sons of Levi:

What kind of offering will the sons of Levi make to fulfil the words of Malachi and John? Logically such a sacrifice as they were authorized to make in the days of their former ministry when they were first called. Will such a sacrifice be offered in the temple? Evidently not in any temple as they are constructed for the work of salvation and exaltation today. It should be remembered that the great temple, which is yet to be built in the City Zion, will not be one edifice, but twelve. Some of these temples will be for the lesser priesthood.

When these temples are built, it is very likely that provision will be made for some ceremonies and ordinances which may be performed by the Aaronic Priesthood and a place provided where the sons of Levi may offer their offering in righteousness. This will have to be the case because all things are to be restored. There were ordinances performed in ancient Israel in the tabernacle when in the wilderness, and after it was established at Shiloh in the land of Canaan, and later in the temple built by Solomon. The Lord has informed us that this was the case and has said that in those edifices ordinances for the people were performed.

These temples that we now have, however, the Lord commanded to be built for the purpose of giving to the saints the blessings which belong to their exaltation, blessings which are to prepare those who receive them to "enter into his rest, . . . which rest is the fulness of his glory," and these ordinances have to be performed by authority of the Melchizedek Priesthood, which the sons of Levi did not hold.[12]

The place of the prince
(Ezekiel 44:1-3)

"Then he brought me back the way of the gate of the outward sanctuary which looketh toward the east; and it was shut. Then said the Lord unto me; This gate shall be shut, it shall not be opened, and no man shall enter in by it; because the Lord, the God of Israel, hath entered in by it, therefore it shall be shut. It is for the prince; the prince, he shall sit in it to eat bread before the Lord; he shall enter by the way of the porch of that gate, and shall go out by the way of the same."

There may be a connection between the entrance for the prince and the holy of holies, where only the high priest went yearly (Hebrews 9:7; Exodus 30:10). It will be a sacred place for only the Lord and his designated servant. Speaking of the Salt Lake Temple, Elder Boyd K. Packer wrote, "Hidden away in the central part of the temple is the Holy of Holies, where the President of the Church may retire when burdened down with heavy decisions to seek an interview with Him whose Church it is. The prophet holds the keys, the spiritual keys and the very literal key to this one door in that sacred edifice."[13]

The rebellious will not enter the house (Ezekiel 44:4–9)

Then brought he me the way of the north gate before the house: and I looked, and, behold, the glory of the Lord filled the house of the Lord: and I fell upon my face.

And the Lord said unto me, Son of man, mark well, and behold with thine eyes, and hear with thine ears all that I say unto thee concerning all the ordinances of the house of the Lord, and all the laws thereof; and mark well the entering in of the house, with every going forth of the sanctuary.

And thou shalt say to the rebellious, even to the house of Israel, Thus saith the Lord God; O ye house of Israel, let it suffice you of all your abominations,

In that ye have brought into my sanctuary strangers, uncircumcised in heart, and uncircumcised in flesh, to be in my sanctuary, to pollute it, even my house, when ye offer my bread, the fat and the blood, and they have broken my covenant because of all your abominations.

And ye have not kept the charge of mine holy things: but ye have set keepers of my charge in my sanctuary for yourselves.

Thus saith the Lord God: No stranger, uncircumcised in heart, nor uncircumcised in flesh, shall enter into my sanctuary, of any stranger that is among the children of Israel.

After seeing the temple filled with the glory of the Lord (44:4), Ezekiel is told that the rebellious of the house of Israel will not enter the Lord's house. The temple to be built in Jerusalem is not to be defiled (43:7). It will be built before the Second Coming, and these verses place restrictions on the unworthy. The same promises given to the Kirtland temple, and all subsequent temples, will be in force: "And inasmuch as my people build a house unto me in the name of the Lord, and do not suffer any unclean thing to come into it, that it be not defiled, my glory shall rest upon it; Yea, and my presence shall be there, for I will come into it, and all the pure in heart that shall come into it shall see God. But if it be defiled I will not come into it, and my glory shall not be there; for I will not come into unholy temples" (D&C 97:15–17).

The priests minister unto the Lord
(Ezekiel 44:15–16)

But the priests the Levites, the sons of Zadok, that kept the charge of my sanctuary when the children of Israel went astray from me, they shall come near to me to minister unto me, and they shall stand before me to offer unto me the fat and the blood, saith the Lord God. They shall enter into my sanctuary, and they shall come near to my table, to minister unto me, and they shall keep my charge.

Zadok was a son of Eleazar, son of Aaron, to whom the office of high priest belongs. The literal sons of Aaron "have a legal right to the bishopric, if they are the firstborn among the sons of Aaron" (D&C 68:16). The office is hereditary (see D&C 68:17–18; 107:69–71). The designation of Aaron's descendants to perform sacrifices in the latter-day temple may also be a fulfillment of the prophecy that all things will be restored in the dispensation of the fullness of times, and/or the time when the office of Presiding Bishop will be filled by legal inheritance.

Clothed with linen garments
(Ezekiel 44:17–19)

And it shall come to pass, that when they enter in at the gates of the inner court, they shall be clothed with linen garments; and no wool shall come upon them, whiles they minister in the gates of the inner court, and within.

They shall have linen bonnets upon their heads, and shall have linen breeches upon their loins; they shall not gird themselves with any thing that causeth sweat.

And when they go forth into the utter court, even into

the utter court to the people, they shall put off their garments wherein they ministered, and lay them in the holy chambers, and they shall put on other garments; and they shall not sanctify the people with their garments.

Again we call attention to the special clothing worn by the priests or administrators in the temple. The verses that follow but are not quoted above also give guidelines for not allowing the temple to be desecrated (44:20–31).

Water issues from under the temple (Ezekiel 47:1, 8-12)

Afterward he brought me again unto the door of the house; and, behold, waters issued out from under the threshold of the house eastward: for the forefront of the house stood toward the east, and the waters came down from under from the right side of the house, at the south side of the altar. . . .

Then said he unto me, These waters issue out toward the east country, and go down into the desert, and go into the sea: which being brought forth into the sea, the waters shall be healed.

And it shall come to pass, that every thing that liveth, which moveth, whithersoever the rivers shall come, shall live: and there shall be a very great multitude of fish, because these waters shall come thither: for they shall be healed; and every thing shall live whither the river cometh.

And it shall come to pass, that the fishers shall stand upon it from En-gedi even unto En-eglaim; they shall be a place to spread forth nets; their fish shall be according to their kinds, as the fish of the great sea, exceeding many.

But the miry places thereof and the marishes thereof shall not be healed; they shall be given to salt.

And by the river upon the bank thereof, on this side and on that side, shall grow all trees for meat, whose leaf shall not fade, neither shall the fruit thereof be consumed: it shall bring forth new fruit according to his months, because their waters they issued out of the sanctuary: and the fruit thereof shall be for meat, and the leaf thereof for medicine.

The waters coming out from under the temple was prophesied by two other prophets. The prophet Joel said: "And it shall come to pass in that day, that the mountains shall drop down new wine, and the hills shall flow with milk, and all the rivers of Judah shall flow with waters, and a fountain shall come forth of the house of the Lord, and shall water the valley Shittim" (Joel 3:18). The prophet Zechariah was more explicit and said it would happen in conjunction with the Lord appearing on the Mount of Olives:

> And his feet shall stand in that day upon the mount of Olives, which is before Jerusalem on the east, and the mount of Olives shall cleave in the midst thereof toward the east and toward the west, and there shall be a very great valley; and half of the mountain shall remove toward the north, and half of it toward the south.
>
> And ye shall flee to the valley of the mountains; for the valley of the mountains shall reach unto Azal: yea, ye shall flee, like as ye fled from before the earthquake in the days of Uzziah king of Judah: and the Lord my God shall come, and all the saints with thee.
>
> And it shall come to pass in that day, that the light shall not be clear, nor dark:
>
> But it shall be one day which shall be known to the Lord, not day, nor night: but it shall come to pass, that at evening time it shall be light.
>
> And it shall be in that day, that living waters shall go out from Jerusalem; half of them toward the former sea, and half of them toward the hinder sea: in summer and in winter shall it be.
>
> And the Lord shall be king over all the earth: in that day shall there be one Lord, and his name one. (Zechariah 14:4–9)

The Prophet Joseph Smith also recognized the literalness of these prophecies and made this declaration:

> Judah must return, Jerusalem must be rebuilt, and the temple, and water come out from under the temple, and the waters of the Dead Sea be healed. It will take some time to rebuild the walls of the city and the temple, &c; and all this must be done before the Son of Man will make His appearance. There will be wars and rumors of wars, signs in the heavens above and on the earth beneath, the sun turned into darkness and the moon to blood, earthquakes in divers places, the seas heaving beyond their bounds; then will appear one grand sign of the Son of Man in heaven. But what will the world do? They

will say it is a planet, a comet, etc. But the Son of man will come as the sign of the coming of the Son of Man, which will be as the light of the morning cometh out of the east.[14]

Elder George A. Smith, commenting on his visit to Jerusalem, observed:

> We read in the 47th chap. of Ezekiel, that living waters were to come out from Jerusalem, and that they should run toward the east; and that the Prophet saw a man with a measuring line in his hand. He measured a thousand cubits, and the water was to his ankles; he measured another thousand, and it was to his knees; another thousand, and it was to his loins; another thousand, and it was a river with waters to swim in, that could not be passed over. He goes on and describes this as something that should take place at Jerusalem. I could but reflect, when standing on the Mount of Olives, on the saying concerning it in the last chapter of Zechariah, where, in speaking of the coming of the Savior, it says his feet shall stand on the Mount of Olives, which is before Jerusalem to the east, and the mount shall cleave in the midst thereof, half going toward the north, and half toward the south. There shall be a very great valley, and the land shall be turned into a plain from Geba to Rimmon, south of Jerusalem, and shall be lifted up, and men shall dwell on it. The same Prophet tells us that living waters shall come out of Jerusalem, half toward the former sea, and half toward the hinder sea, and that in summer and in winter shall it be.
>
> The covenant at Mar Saba is situated on the canon, which is the outlet of the brook Kedron; but it was perfectly dry when we were there, not a drop of water running in it. There are seasons of the year, I suppose, when waters run there, but these prophecies declare that living waters shall run out of Jerusalem in summer and winter, and I am foolish enough to believe that they will be literally fulfilled.[15]

The Dead Sea is dead because there is no outlet, and it is the lowest spot on earth. The earthquake mentioned by Zechariah will apparently change that situation. There will be waters which can support fish. To those who wonder about what will be eaten during the Millennium, the twelfth verse speaks of trees that will bear "fruit for meat, and the leaf thereof for medicine."

The New Testament description of Jerusalem also mentions the water coming out from the throne of God, which is in the temple, but has some variations from the Old Testament accounts:

> And he shewed me a pure river of water of life, clear as crystal, proceeding out of the throne of God and of the Lamb.
>
> In the midst of the street of it, and on either side of the river, was there the tree of life, which bare twelve manner of fruits, and yielded her fruit every month: and the leaves of the tree were for the healing of the nations.
>
> And there shall be no more curse: but the throne of God and of the Lamb shall be in it; and his servants shall serve him. (Revelation 22:1–3).

We will learn more of these changes to the land and the water when the Millennium comes.

Summary of Chapters 40–44; 47:1–12

The gathering of the Lord's people in the latter days is well under way, and the building of His temples is being accelerated to accommodate the large gathering that is yet to take place. The temple at Jerusalem shown in vision to Ezekiel has not yet been built. However, the physical gathering of Judah to that land is well under way. In the Lord's due time, the temple in Jerusalem will be built, and then the prophecies spoken of by Ezekiel in these chapters will be verified.

Notes

1. Joseph Smith, *Teachings of the Prophet Joseph Smith,* sel. Joseph Fielding Smith (Salt Lake City: Deseret Book, 1976), 308.

2. See John B. Taylor, *Ezekiel: An Introduction and Commentary, Tyndale Old Testament Commentaries* (Downer's Grove, Ill.: InterVarsity Press, 1969), 20:250–54.

3. Smith, *Teachings,* 172–73.

4. Bruce R. McConkie, *The Mortal Messiah* (Salt Lake City: Deseret Book, 1979), 1:121.

5. Boyd K. Packer, *The Holy Temple* (Salt Lake City: Deseret Book, 1980), 72.

6. Bruce R. McConkie, *The Millennial Messiah* (Salt Lake City: Deseret Book, 1982), 599–600.

7. McConkie, *The Mortal Messiah,* 1:121

8. Orson Pratt, in *Journal of Discourses*, 26 vols. (London: Latter-day Saints' Book Depot, 1854–86), 14:350–51.

9. Joseph Smith, *History of The Church of Jesus Christ of Latter-day Saints*, ed. B. H. Roberts, 2d ed. rev., 7 vols. (Salt Lake City: The Church of Jesus Christ of Latter-day Saints, 1932–51), 2:428.

10. James E. Talmage, *House of the Lord* (Salt Lake City: Deseret Book, 1969), 37–38.

11. Smith, *Teachings*, 173.

12. Joseph Fielding Smith, *Doctrines of Salvation*, comp. Bruce R. McConkie, 3 vols. (Salt Lake City: Bookcraft, 1956), 3:93–94.

13. Packer, *The Holy Temple*, 4.

14. Smith, *Teachings*, 286–87.

15. George A. Smith, in *Journal of Discourses*, 286–87.

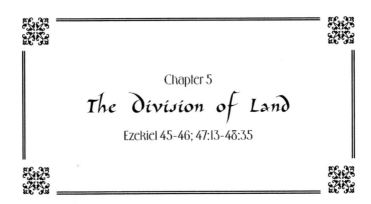

Chapter 5

The Division of Land

Ezekiel 45-46; 47:13-48:35

braham was given the land "from the river in Egypt unto the great river, the river Euphrates" for his seed (Genesis 15:18). This land was never fully occupied under one head but will be someday. After the house of Israel was taken into Egypt, Moses led them out to occupy the land "from the Red Sea even unto the sea of the Philistines, and from the desert unto the river" (Exodus 23:31–33). Due to their iniquities, the promised land has been forfeited from time to time. The land has been promised to Abraham's descendants again in the last days. Abraham's descendants number in the millions. Only some of these have had designated areas given to them, but the others will certainly be given their portions.

When Joshua conquered the land of Canaan, the land was divided among the various tribes of Israel. Cities were designated for the Levites to live in all of the twelve tribes' territories (see Joshua 13–21). The same process of land distribution for the latter days was shown to Ezekiel, although the territories are not correlated with those given in Joshua's day. Again, the significance of the division and the location of the territories will be understood in the day of their fulfillment.

The divisions as shown to Ezekiel are outlined below.

1. Ezekiel 45. The Lord designates a holy portion of the land.
   a. A portion for the sanctuary (45:2–3).
   b. A portion for the priests, the ministers of the sanctuary, and a portion for the Levites (45:4–5).
   c. A portion adjacent to the holy portion for the whole house of Israel (45:6).
   d. The princes portion. The princes will no more oppress the Lord's people (45:7–8).
   e. The requirements and responsibilities for the princes (45:9–17).
   f. The dates of certain offerings to be carried out by the priests (45:18–25).
2. Ezekiel 46:1–24. The gates of the inner court that looks toward the east shall be shut except on the Sabbat.
   a. The prince shall enter the east gate; the priests will prepare the sacrifice for the priest to make unto the Lord (46:2–8).
   b. The people who enter from the north shall exit by the south and vice versa. An offering will be prepared by the prince (46:9–15).
   c. The prince is given guidelines for gifts and inheritances (46:16–18).
   d. Ezekiel is shown where the priests make their offerings (46:19–24).
3. Ezekiel 47:13–23. The borders of the land which the twelve tribes of Israel will inherit.
   a. Joseph will have two portions (47:13).
   b. The borders of the land for all the tribes are designated (47:14–21).
   c. Strangers will have inheritance in the tribe where they live and raise their children (47:22–23).
4. Ezekiel 48:1–29. The names of the tribes and their portions are listed.
   a. A portion for Dan (48:1).
   b. A portion for Asher (48:2).
   c. A portion for Nephtali (48:3).
   d. A portion for Manassah (48:4).
   e. A portion for Ephraim (48:5).
   f. A portion for Reuben (48:6)
   g. A portion for Judah (48:7).

     h. The oblation unto the Lord for the priests, the sons of Zadok who are sanctified (48:8–12).

     i. The oblation unto the Lord for the Levites which will not be sold (48:13–20).

     j. The residue for the prince (48:21–22).

     k. A portion for Benjamin (48:23).

     l. A portion for Simeon (48:24).

     m. A portion for Issachar (48:25).

     n. A portion for Zebulun (48:26).

     o. A portion for Gad (48:27).

     p. The border of the land is to be divided (48:28–29).

5. Ezekiel 48:30–34. The gates of the city are named after the tribes of Israel.

     a. Three gates on the north: Reuben, Judah, and Levi (48:31).

     b. Three gates on the east: Joseph, Benjamin, and Dan (48:32).

     c. Three gates on the south: Simeon, Issachar, and Zebulun (48:33).

     d. Three gates on the west: Gad, Asher, and Naphtali (48:34).

6. JST, Ezekiel 48:35. The name of the city will be "Holy; for the Lord shall be there."

Notes and Commentary

As expected, general authorities have made few comments on these chapters. The Prophet Joseph Smith did make one change in his translation of the Bible (48:35), but no other comments are found in his teachings. There are a few modern-day scriptures that are applicable to help us understand the general message. Again, because of the nature of the text, there will be no quotations or comments on many verses.

The prince shall enter by way of the porch
(Ezekiel 46:1–2)

Thus saith the Lord God; The gate of the inner court that looketh toward the east shall be shut the six working days; but on the sabbath it shall be opened, and in the day of the new moon it shall be opened. And the prince shall enter by the way of the porch of that gate without, and shall stand by the post of the gate, and the priests shall prepare his burnt offering and his peace offerings, and he shall worship at the threshold of the gate: then he shall go forth; but the gate shall not be shut until the evening.

The opening of the inner east gate only on the Sabbath is not the pattern followed in modern-day temples. Further revelation is needed and will be given to understand this chapter when the time is appropriate.

The Division of the land
(Ezekiel 47:13–48:35)

Elder Parley P. Pratt made this observation concerning the overall plan of the Lord's division of the land.

> The Lord God has revealed through Ezekiel the prophet a plan for the survey and division of Palestine to the Twelve Tribes of Israel on their return to the land of their fathers; also for laying out the new city of Jerusalem, with its squares, blocks, public grounds, and suburbs, and its temple.
>
> Thus theology includes the surveyor's art and the planning of cities, as well as temples, and shows that these arts are cultivated in heaven, and that the very highest Intelligence of the Heaven of heavens stoops, or condescends, to grace these arts by his own particular attention and example.[1]

When Moroni abridged the Jaredite record, he paraphrased Ether's words concerning Jerusalem becoming a holy city unto the Lord (Ether 13:5) and also concerning the New Jerusalem being built in "this land" of America (Ether 13:6–10). Moroni further paraphrased Ether concerning Jerusalem: "And then also cometh the Jerusalem of old; and the inhabitants thereof, blessed are they, for they have been washed in the blood of the Lamb; and they are they who were scattered and gathered in from the four quarters of the earth, and from the north countries, and are partakers of the fulfilling of the covenant which God made with their father, Abraham" (Ether 13:11). Those "gathered . . . from the north countries" has reference to the ten tribes who were taken captive by Assyria in 721 b.c., and then traveled into the North. Moses delivered the keys of "the leading of the ten tribes from the land of the north" to Joseph Smith and Oliver Cowdery in the Kirtland temple (D&C 110:11; see also Articles of Faith 10). Thus, Ezekiel's vision, showing that all twelve tribes shall receive an inheritance according to the land given to their fathers, is consistent with the keys Moses gave to Joseph Smith. The ten tribes will apparently come to both the New Jerusalem and the Old Jerusalem.

As quoted in the previous chapters, the returning sons of Levi will make a literal sacrifice as part of the restoration of all things in the dispensation of the fulness of times.[2] Those coming from the north countries are to be "crowned with glory, even in Zion, by the hands of the servants of the Lord, even the children of Ephraim" (D&C 133:32; see also vv. 26–34). The Lord then reveals blessings to Ephraim: "Behold, this is the blessing of the everlasting God upon the tribes of Israel, and the richer blessing upon the head of Ephraim and his fellows" (D&C 133:34).

As the bishop in Zion, Edward Partridge was given the responsibility to divide the lands in Zion: "And whoso standeth in this mission is appointed to be a judge in Israel, like as it was in ancient days, to divide the lands of the heritage of God unto his children" (D&C 58:17; see also 57:7; 51:1–4). The bishop in Jerusalem should have the same responsibility.

Joseph will have two portions
(Ezekiel 47:13, 21)

Thus saith the Lord God; This shall be the border, whereby ye shall inherit the land according to the twelve tribes of Israel: Joseph shall have two portions. . . . So shall ye divide this land unto you according to the tribes of Israel.

The two portions mentioned above may have reference to Joseph's two sons, Ephraim and Manasseh, each receiving a portion, or it may mean that one or each of them will receive a double portion. The majority of the Church members today are from the tribe of Ephraim, and there are many among the millions of Lamanites today who are from both Ephraim and Manasseh. It seems that most of these would reside in America, but perhaps there are also many more people of these tribes in the eastern hemisphere than of the other tribes.

There will be no comment upon the dimensions of the land (Ezekiel 48:14–21) because it is unfamiliar to most readers.

Strangers to have an inheritance
(Ezekiel 47:22–23)

And it shall come to pass, that ye shall divide it by lot for an inheritance unto you, and to the strangers that sojourn among you, which shall beget children among you: and they shall be unto you as born in the country among the children of Israel; they shall have inheritance with you among the tribes of Israel. And it shall come to pass, that in what tribe the stranger sojourneth, there shall ye give him his inheritance, saith the Lord God.

The strangers who reside among the tribes of Israel are apparently Gentiles or "heathens" who have joined the Church and, thus, are adopted into the house of Israel: "And I will bless them through thy name; for as many as receive this Gospel shall be called after thy name, and shall be accounted thy seed, and shall rise up and bless thee, as their father" (Abraham 2:10; see also D&C 84:32–34). As quoted previously, "the heathen nations" are equated with "the house of Joseph" when they accept "the gospel of their salvation" (D&C 90:10–11).

The name of the city
(Ezekiel 48:35 JST)

It was round about eighteen thousand measures; and the name of the city from that day shall be called Holy; for the Lord shall be there.

When a temple is built in Jerusalem unto the Lord, "the Son of Man [will] have a place to manifest himself to his people" (D&C 109:5). This is also the conclusion of the vision given to Ezekiel and the end of his writings.

Summary of Ezekiel Chapters 45-48

Most, if not all, of the things shown to Ezekiel in these chapters are yet to happen, but the Lord gave the pattern to Ezekiel, and it will be followed as the eternal destiny of the twelve tribes unfolds. Nephi said concerning Isaiah: "In the days that the prophecies of Isaiah shall be fulfilled men shall know of a surety, at the times when they shall come to pass" (2 Nephi 25:7). The same is certainly true for the prophecies of Ezekiel. It will be interesting to see them unfold before our eyes.

Summary of the book of Ezekiel

The book of Ezekiel, except for a few passages, does not seem to be well known to members of The Church of Jesus Christ of Latter-day Saints. As observed from this writer's personal study, except for chapter 37 on the two sticks, chapters 18 and 33 on man's accountability, and a few other occasional references, it has rarely been quoted, paraphrased, or alluded to in general conferences of the Church and other public meetings, at least when the messages have been recorded. It has been written about even less. Elder Bruce R. McConkie is the only modern-day apostle who has written extensively on much of Ezekiel's apocalyptic passages.

I hope this section will inspire others to follow the Savior's admonition to "search the prophets, for many there be that testify of these things" (3 Nephi 23:5), and many will come to understand and appreciate this great prophet.

Notes
1. Parley P. Pratt, *Key to the Science of Theology* (Salt Lake City: Deseret Book, 1978), 2–3.
2. Joseph Smith, *Teachings of the Prophet Joseph Smith*, sel. Joseph Fielding Smith (Salt Lake City: Deseret Book, 1976), 173; see also Ephesians 1:9–10.

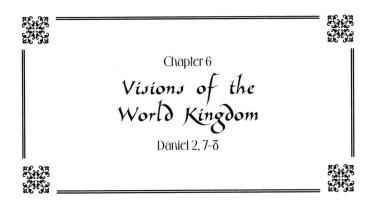

Chapter 6

Visions of the World Kingdom

Daniel 2, 7-8

he book of Daniel is divided quite naturally into two sections: the faith-promoting accounts of Daniel and his three friends found in the first six chapters and four visions of the future shown to and interpreted by Daniel (although the second chapter also gives Daniel's interpretation of King Nebuchadnezzar's dream). Are these literal and authentic accounts or just edifying traditional folklore that was handed down and finally collected, written, and accepted by the Jewish community?

The authorship of Daniel is highly questioned and looked upon in the scholarly biblical world as the latter theory mentioned above. Scholars believe that it was written probably around the first or second century b.c. The fact that it was not part of the prophets in the Jewish canon but was among the less sacred writings is one consideration—but not the only one—for the acceptance of this theory.[1] However, other biblical scholars argue that Daniel is the author.

The book mentions Daniel as its author in several passages, such as 9:2 and 10:2. That Jesus concurred is clear from his reference to "the abomination of desolation, spoken of by Daniel the prophet" (Matthew 24:15; see Daniel 9:27; 11:31; 12:11). The book was probably completed circa 530 B.C., shortly after the capture of Babylon by Cyrus in 539 B.C.

The widely held view that the book of Daniel is largely fiction rests mainly on the modern philosophical assumption that long-range predictive prophecy is impossible. Therefore, all fulfilled predictions in Daniel, it is claimed, had to have been composed no earlier than the Maccabean period (200 B.C.)—after their fulfillment had taken place. But objective evidence excludes this hypothesis on several counts.[2]

Scholars then give their arguments for the four kingdoms seen by Daniel to be Babylon, Medes-Persia, Greece, and Rome, rather than counting Medes-Persia as two kingdoms to the exclusion of Rome, as do fictional theorists. The above authors cite the language as a second argument and the fulfillment of prophecy as a third. I accept the latter position of the scholars who argue that Daniel is the author. After all, in addition to the fact that Jesus refers to Daniel as a prophet, the Doctrine and Covenants does also (see D&C 116). Furthermore, another revelation given to Joseph Smith directly quotes from Daniel's prophecy in Daniel 2 regarding the stone cut out of the mountain and explains that the stone is the latter-day kingdom (see D&C 65). There is more than sufficient evidence to accept the book of Daniel as authentic.[3]

Does Jehovah (Jesus Christ) know the end from the beginning? All of the standard works bear testimony that he does. The Old Testament contains this testimony in the book of Isaiah (Isaiah 46:9–10). In the New Testament, the Lord identified himself to John the Revelator as "Alpha and Omega, the beginning and the end" (Revelation 21:6). In Abraham, once a part of the Old Testament but now in the Pearl of Great Price, we read, "My name is Jehovah, and I know the end from the beginning; therefore my hand shall be over thee" (Abraham 2:8). Based on His foreknowledge of all things, He covenanted with Abraham and his seed (Abraham 2:9–11; see also Genesis 18:17–19).

In the Book of Mormon, Jacob, Nephi's brother, bore testimony that Christ's knowledge of all things was the attribute that enabled him to atone for our sins (2 Nephi 9:20–22). "The Lord your God, even Jesus Christ, the Great I Am, Alpha and Omega, the beginning and the end" revealed to the Prophet Joseph Smith that he "knoweth all things, for all things are present before [his] eyes" (D&C 38:1–2). The Prophet declared that "the past, the present, and the future were and are, with Him [the Great Jehovah], one eternal 'now.'"[4]

With these testimonies before their eyes, some want to cry "predestination." In answer, I quote what was attributed to the Prophet Joseph Smith by a member of congress. The Prophet testified in Washington, D.C., seeking redress for the suffering of the Saints in Missouri: "I believe that God foreknew everything, but did not foreordain everything; I deny that foreordain and foreknow is the same thing."[5] Man has his agency and, thus, God, with his foreknowledge, has programmed the earth to bring about his purposes by compensating for the evil actions of men which he foreknew would but did not cause to happen. Thus, the Lord's declarative question to Joseph: "Do I not hold the destinies of all the armies of the nations of the earth?" (D&C 117:6).

The vision of king Nebuchadnezzar, which Daniel interprets in the second chapter of the book of Daniel, is widely known in the Christian world and in the Church. The Christian world generally interprets the vision as being fulfilled in the establishment of the Christian church in the meridian of time. A few of the churches recognize the vision as a latter-day fulfillment (i.e., Seventh Day Adventists) and see themselves fulfilling it. The leaders of The Church of Jesus Christ of Latter-day Saints have consistently claimed the vision is an interpretation of the kingdoms of the world up to the time of the Restoration, at which time the God of heaven set up the beginning of His kingdom that was to stand forever.

There are two more visions discussed in this chapter (Daniel 7 and 8), shown to Daniel after he had interpreted King Nebuchadnezzar's dream. These sustain and amplify what was shown to the king. The three visions are outlined below.

1. Daniel 2. King Nebuchadnezzar has a dream which troubles him. He cannot remember the dream but asks his wise men to tell him the dream and the interpretation of it. They cannot do it, but Daniel interprets it by the revelation of God.

    a. The magicians, astrologers, sorcerers, and Chaldeans say they will interpret the dream if he will tell it to them. The king says if they tell him the dream and its interpretation, they will receive gifts, rewards, and honor. If they do not tell him, they will be killed (2:2–9).

    b. The Chaldeans say there is not a man upon the earth who can do as the king requests. The king is angry and commands all the wise men of Babylon to be destroyed, including Daniel and his fellows (2:10–13).

c. Daniel goes to the king and says he will give the interpretation if he is given time. He consults with his three friends and asks for their support (2:14–18).

d. The interpretation of the dream is revealed to Daniel, and he acknowledges the wisdom and might of God. He praises and thanks God (2:19–23).

e. Daniel is taken to the king and tells him the God of heaven reveals secrets of what will be in the latter days, not because of his (Daniel's) wisdom, but for the sake of the living (2:24–30).

f. Daniel tells the king his dream was of a great image with a head of gold, breast and arms of silver, belly and thighs of brass, legs of iron, and feet of part iron and part clay. A stone cut out of the mountain without hands "smote the image upon his feet" and broke them in pieces; the stone became a great mountain and filled the whole earth (2:31–35).

g. Daniel interprets the dream. Nebuchadnezzar is the head of gold, or the kingdom of Babylon that God had given him. Another kingdom inferior to Nebuchadnezzar (silver) will arise and defeat Babylon, and then a third kingdom of brass will rule over all the earth. A fourth kingdom, strong as iron, will subdue all things and rule, then "break in pieces and bruise." The iron kingdom will be divided, like the toes of the feet, and "be partly strong and partly broken; "the divided parts of the iron kingdom will "not cleave one to another" (2:36–43).

h. In the days of the those kings, the God of heaven will "set up a kingdom which will never be destroyed," but will stand forever (2:44–45).

i. The king worships Daniel and acknowledges that Daniel's "God is God of gods." Daniel is given gifts and made ruler over all the governors and wise men of Babylon. Daniel requests that his three friends be placed over the affairs of Babylon (2:46–49).

2. Daniel 7. Daniel has a dream and writes it in the first year of Belshezzar, king of Babylon.

   a. Four great beasts come up out of the sea (7:2–3).

      1. The first is like a lion with eagle wings, and a man's heart is given to it (7:4).

      2. The second is like a bear. It has three ribs in its mouth and devours much flesh (7:5).

      3. The third is like a leopard. It has four fowl wings and four heads; dominion is given to it (7:6).

      4. The fourth is strong and terrible with great iron teeth that devour and broke in pieces the third beast and stamps the residue with its feet. It has ten horns. Another little horn comes up among the ten horns and plucks up three of them by the roots. The little horn has eyes and a mouth (7:7–8).

   b. The thrones are cast down and the Ancient of Days sits. Thousands minister unto him, and ten thousand times ten thousand are judged out of the books. The beast is slain and burned. The other beasts have their dominion taken away, but their lives are prolonged "for a season and time" (7:9–12).

   c. One like the Son of Man comes with the clouds of heaven unto the Ancient of Days. He is given everlasting dominion, glory, and a kingdom that will not be destroyed (7:13–14).

   d. One who stands by gives Daniel the interpretation. The four beasts are four kings that will arise out of the earth. The Saints of the Most High will take the kingdom and possess it forever (7:15–18).

   e. The little horn that comes among the ten horns of the fourth beast makes war with the Saints and prevails against them until the Ancient of Days comes and judgment is given to the Saints of the

Most High. The Saints eventually possess the kingdom (7:19–22).

    f. The fourth kingdom is diverse from all kingdoms and will devour the earth. The ten horns are ten kings that will arise out of the fourth kingdom. The little horn is another king that will subdue three kings. He will "speak great words against the Most High, . . . wear out the Saints," and change laws. But judgment will take away his dominion. The kingdom shall be given to the "Saints of the Most High." Daniel is troubled (7:23–28).

3. Daniel 8. In the third year of Belshazzar, Daniel has another vision. He is at Shushan in the palace, in the province of Elam by the river Ulai.

    a. Daniel sees a ram with two horns, one higher than the other, the higher one coming up last. The ram pushes westward, northward, and southward; no beast can stand before him. He becomes great (8:3–4).

    b. A he goat from the west with a notable horn between his eyes runs into the ram and breaks the two horns (8:5–7).

    c. The great horn is broken, and four notable horns come up. Out of one of the four horns comes a little horn that takes away the daily sacrifice and casts truth to the ground (8:8–12).

    d. One Saint tells another that the period the dream covers will be two thousand and three hundred days; then the sanctuary will be cleansed (8:13–14).

    e. Gabriel interprets the vision for Daniel. The ram with two horns represents the kings of Media and Persia. The rough goat represents the country of Grecia, and the horn between his eyes is the first king of Greece. The four notable ones that stand up are "four kingdoms [that] shall stand up out of the nation, but not in his power." In the latter time of the four kingdoms, a fierce king shall stand up and "destroy the mighty and the holy people." He "shall stand up against the Prince of princes; but he shall be broken" (8:15–26).

f. Daniel is sick but does the king's business. He is astonished at the vision, but no one understands it (8:27).

Notes and Commentary

Daniel chapter two is one of the better known passages of scripture in the Old Testament to Latter-day Saints. It is one of the passages most quoted and referred to in general conferences. The Prophet Joseph Smith mentioned chapter two and chapter seven repeatedly in his sermons and writings. However, he did not make any changes in the Joseph Smith Translation to the chapters discussed in this section of this book. There are several significant revelations in the Doctrine and Covenants that give us help in interpreting these chapters. Although there are not as many references to chapter eight, Latter-day Saint sources help us understand the three chapters of Daniel under consideration here.

Since many of the comments of Church leaders are general and/or repetitious, those selected for inclusion here are those which offer some unique insights.

Nebuchadnezzar's dream
(Daniel 2:1)

And in the second year of the reign of Nebuchadnezzar, Nebuchadnezzar dreamed dreams, wherewith his spirit was troubled, and his sleep brake from him.

Some see a contradiction between the three years of special provisions for the select children of Israel (Daniel 1:5), and the date Daniel interpreted the king's dream in the second year of Nebuchadnezzar's reign. However, the first chapter of Daniel implies that he could have interpreted the dream during the three years of the special diet: "Daniel had understanding in all visions and dreams" (1:17) during these three years. The following verse states that "at the end of the days . . . the prince of the eunuchs brought them in" (1:18). If chapter one is chronological, there is no contradiction. Chapter 2 goes back to the second year of King Nebuchadnezzar's reign to give the evidence of Daniel interpreting dreams during the three years of special provisions.

Daniel seeks an interpretation
(Daniel 2:2–13)

Then the king commanded to call the magicians, and the astrologers, and the sorcerers, and the Chaldeans, for to shew the king his dreams. So they came and stood before the king.

And the king said unto them, I have dreamed a dream, and my spirit was troubled to know the dream.

Then spake the Chaldeans to the king in Syriack, O king, live for ever: tell thy servants the dream, and we will shew the interpretation,

The king answered and said to the Chaldeans, The thing is gone from me: if ye will not make known unto me the dream, with the interpretation thereof, ye shall be cut in pieces, and your houses shall be made a dunghill.

But if ye shew the dream, and the interpretation thereof, ye shall receive of me gifts and rewards and great honour: therefore shew me the dream, and the interpretation thereof.

They answered again and said, Let the king tell his servants the dream, and we will shew the interpretation of it. The king answered and said, I know of certainty that ye would gain the time, because ye see the thing is gone from me.

But if ye will not make known unto me the dream, there is but one decree for you: for ye have prepared lying and corrupt words to speak before me, till the time be changed: therefore tell me the dream, and I shall know that ye can shew me the interpretation thereof.

The Chaldeans answered before the king, and said, There is not a man upon the earth that can shew the king's matter: therefore there is no king, lord, nor ruler, that asked such things at any magician, or astrologer, or Chaldean.

And it is a rare thing that the king requireth, and there is none other that can shew it before the king, except the gods, whose dwelling is not with flesh.

For this cause the king was angry and very furious, and commanded to destroy all the wise men of Babylon. And the decree went forth that the wise men should be slain; and they sought Daniel and his fellows to be slain.

The task given to the wise men of Babylon seems impossible, and the response of the wise men is certainly reasonable (2:7, 10–11).

However, we sense that the king lacks trust in these men. "Till the time be changed" (2:9) suggests they would ask for more time. Apparently they had used lies and deceit to appease his requests in the past (2:9, 12), but that should not surprise us as we study world powers devoid of the Spirit of the Lord. Daniel and his three friends being included in the king's decree was probably not initiated by the king but by the captain of the king's guard because the king had given a general command to destroy all the wise men. Nonetheless, it gave the Lord an opportunity to show the king that the God of heaven knows all and reveals his will to man through his servants the prophets (JST, Amos 3:6–7).

Writing in Aramaic
(Daniel 2:4–7:28)

These chapters, beginning at 2:4, are written in Aramaic, while the rest of the book is written in Hebrew. The writing in two languages is unique to this book in the Bible. The exact reason is not known, but two suggestions are given below.

The Anchor Bible suggests that "all twelve chapters had originally been composed in Aramaic. But in order to ensure that the book would receive canonical recognition, the beginning (1:1–2:4a) and end (chapters 8–12) were translated into Hebrew.[6] Furthermore, it suggests that "the writer who translated into Hebrew the Aramaic original of the book found this point in verse 4 a convenient and 'logical' place to stop his work of translation, since it seemed only natural to let the 'Chaldeans' speak in their own language. The translator resumed his work at the beginning of chapter 8 and rendered the remainder of the work in Hebrew."[7]

The NIV Study Bible proposes that "these six chapters deal with matters of importance to the Gentile nations of the Near East and were written in a language understandable to all. But the last five chapters (8–12) revert to Hebrew, since they deal with special concerns of the chosen people."[8]

Daniel is given the interpretation of the dream
(Daniel 2:14–23)

Then Daniel answered with counsel and wisdom to Arioch the captain of the king's guard, which was gone forth to slay the wise men of Babylon: He answered and said to Arioch the king's captain, Why is the decree so hasty from the king? Then Arioch made the thing known to Daniel.

Then Daniel went in, and desired of the king that he would give him time, and that he would shew the king the interpretation Then Daniel went to his house, and made the thing known to Hananiah, Mishael, and Azariah, his companions: That they would desire mercies of the God of heaven concerning this secret; that Daniel and his fellows should not perish with the rest of the wise men of Babylon.

Then was the secret revealed unto Daniel in a night vision. Then Daniel blessed the God of heaven. Daniel answered and said, Blessed be the name of God for ever and ever: for wisdom and might are his: And he changeth the times and the seasons: he removeth kings, and setteth up kings: he giveth wisdom unto the wise, and knowledge to them that know understanding: He revealeth the deep and secret things: he knoweth what is in the darkness, and the light dwelleth with him.

I thank thee, and praise thee, O thou God of my fathers, who hast given me wisdom and might, and hast made known unto me now what we desired of thee: for thou hast now made known unto us the king's matter.

Daniel's courage was exemplified by going to the king to seek some time to obtain a revelation. Note that he also sought the faith and supporting strength of his three friends (2:17). Furthermore, his faith was shown as he recognized the power and attributes of God in his praise of him after "the secret [was] revealed unto Daniel in a night vision" (2:19–23).

In a revelation given to the Prophet Joseph Smith as he wrote to the Saints while he was in prison, the Lord uses language similar to the language Daniel used in his praise of the Lord. "And also that God hath set his hand and seal to change the times and seasons, and to blind their minds, that they may not understand his marvelous workings; that he may prove them also and take them in their own craftiness" (D&C 121:12; see also Daniel 2:6–15).

Does the Lord's use of these words not suggest that the Lord was allowing the corruption of the Saints' enemies in Missouri for "a small moment" (121:7), just as he had allowed the corruption in Babylon at the time of Daniel? This seems to be the case.

Daniel 2:21 and Doctrine and Covenants 121:12 are sometimes used to support seasonal changes as a sign of the Second Coming. While there will be drought and famine, the sign of the rainbow is the only specific sign, to my knowledge, which designates a year when the Lord will not come. The Prophet said: "[The Lord] gave a sign and said: In the days of Noah I set a bow in the heavens as a sign and token that in any year that the bow should be seen the Lord would not come; but there should be seed time and harvest during that year: but whenever you see the bow withdrawn, it shall be a token that there shall be famine, pestilence, and great distress among the nations, and that the coming of the Messiah is not far distant."[9]

The God of heaven reveals secrets
(Daniel 2:24–30)

Therefore Daniel went in unto Arioch, whom the king had ordained to destroy the wise men of Babylon: he went and said thus unto him; Destroy not the wise men of Babylon: bring me in before the king, and I will shew unto the king the interpretation.

Then Arioch brought in Daniel before the king in haste, and said thus unto him, I have found a man of the captives of Judah, that will make known unto the king the interpretation.

The king answered and said to Daniel, whose name was Belteshazzar, Art thou able to make known unto me the dream which I have seen, and the interpretation thereof?

Daniel answered in the presence of the king, and said, The secret which the king hath demanded cannot the wise men, the astrologers, the magicians, the soothsayers, shew unto the king;

But there is a God in heaven that revealeth secrets, and maketh known to the king Nebuchadnezzar what shall be in the latter days. Thy dream, and the visions of thy head upon thy bed, are these;

As for thee, O king, thy thoughts came into thy mind upon thy bed, what should come to pass hereafter: and he that revealeth secrets maketh known to thee what shall come to pass.

But as for me, this secret is not revealed to me for any wisdom that I have more than any living, but for their sakes that shall make known the interpretation to the king, and that thou mightest know the thoughts of thy heart.

Daniel reminds the king that his wise men cannot show him the secret demanded and then gives full credit to the God in heaven for the knowledge he was about to impart to the king. The mysteries of God are only known by revelation. President Brigham Young made these observations regarding the power of the Holy Ghost being the source of understanding the things of God:

> I was a Bible reader before I came into this Church; and, so far as the letter of the book was concerned, I understood it. I professed to be a believer in the Bible so far as I knew how; but as for understanding by the Spirit of the Lord, I never did until I became a Latter-day Saint. I had many a time read Daniel's interpretation of Nebuchadnezzar's dream, but it was always a dark subject to me. . . .
>
> We profess to have the light, intelligence, and knowledge with which to understand the things of God. The dream of King Nebuchadnezzar and its interpretation by David are as plain to the man and woman filled with the power of the Holy Ghost, as are the most common lessons to the school-children: they most clearly understand the interpretation. Daniel saw that in the latter days the God of heaven was going to set up his kingdom upon this his earth. He has set that kingdom up, as you who are here this day are witnesses.[10]

A great image of various materials
(Daniel 2:31-35)

Thou, O king, sawest, and behold a great image. This great image, whose brightness was excellent, stood before thee; and the form thereof was terrible. This image's head was of fine gold, his breast and his arms of silver, his belly and his thighs of brass, his legs of iron, his feet part of iron and part of clay. Thou sawest till that a stone was cut out without hands, which smote the image upon his feet that were of iron and clay, and brake them to pieces. Then was the iron, the clay, the brass, the silver, and the gold, broken to pieces together, and became like the chaff of the summer threshingfloors; and the wind carried them away, that no place was found for them: and the stone that smote the image became a great mountain, and filled the whole earth.

Nebuchadnezzar's dream was given to him again by Daniel. That was a miracle that could only come by revelation. The Prophet Joseph Smith rejoiced "that God grants unto the world Seers and Prophets" who "saw the stone cut out of the mountain, which filled the whole earth."[11] The Prophet accepted the text of Daniel as literal, as this and subsequent quotes will show.

Daniel interprets the dream
(Daniel 2:36-43)

This is the dream; and we will tell the interpretation thereof before the king. Thou, O king, art a king of kings: for the God of heaven hath given thee a kingdom, power, and strength, and glory.

And wheresoever the children of men dwell, the beasts of the field and the fowls of the heaven hath he given into thine hand, and hath made thee ruler over them all. Thou art this head of gold.

And after thee shall arise another kingdom inferior to thee, and another third kingdom of brass, which shall bear rule over all the earth. And the fourth kingdom shall be strong as iron: forasmuch as iron breaketh in pieces and subdueth all things: and as iron that breaketh all these, shall it break in pieces and bruise.

And whereas thou sawest the feet and toes, part of potters' clay, and part of iron, the kingdom shall be divided; but there shall be in it of the strength of the iron, forasmuch as thou sawest the iron mixed with miry clay.

And as the toes of the feet were part of iron, and part of clay, so the kingdom shall be partly strong, and partly broken. And whereas thou sawest iron mixed with miry clay, they shall mingle themselves with the seed of men: but they shall not cleave one to another, even as iron is not mixed with clay.

As further evidence of the power of God, Daniel gives the king the interpretation. Daniel only names one of the four kingdoms: that of Nebuchadnezzar, or Babylon. However, many of the latter-day prophets and Apostles have named other kingdoms and nations. Again, all of those who have commented will not be quoted.

The most detailed and complete identification of the kingdoms outlined by Daniel was given by Rudger Clawson, president of the Quorum of the Twelve in 1930.

The Christian world of today is witness of the fact that the very things which the great image stood for have occurred so far as time has gone. History certifies to the fact that King Nebuchadnezzar was the head of gold. The Medes and Persians, an inferior kingdom to Babylon, were the arms and breast of silver. The Macedonian kingdom, under Alexander the Great, was the belly and thighs of brass; and the Roman kingdom under the Caesars was the legs of iron. For mark you, later on the kingdom, or empire of Rome, was divided. The head of the government in one division was at Rome, and the head of the government in the other division was at Constantinople. So these two great divisions represented the legs of iron. Finally, the Roman empire was broken up into smaller kingdoms, represented by the feet and toes of iron and clay, and as there were ten toes on the image we might well conclude that the following ten kingdoms stand to represent the toes: Italy, established in 496 A.D.; France, in 753; England, 853; Germany, 806; Holland, 922; Portugal, 1138; Persia, 1139; Austria-Hungary, 1159; Spain, 1171; Greece, 1829 A.D. The stone cut out of the mountain without hands, representing the kingdom of God, was established April 6th, 1830, with six members, and is known as the Church of Jesus Christ of Latter-day Saints.[12]

While some may question such detail or name slightly differing nations and dates, it is a fairly common outline of the nations prophesied of by Daniel both within and outside of the Church.[13] President Spencer W. Kimball supported the interpretation of the ten toes above. He didn't name the exact same European nations but grouped them together under the title "the days of these kings" (Daniel 2:44).[14]

In another discourse, Elder Orson Pratt identified the four world powers and the ten toes the same as the quote above and also gave sound argument for why the kingdom set up without hands could not be the Church or kingdom set up at the first advent of the Messiah. He included evidence from Daniel chapter 7 in both discourses.[15]

In a more recent and, thus, more available source, Elder Bruce R. McConkie also designated the four major kingdoms as named above and the iron and clay feet as "the numerous, divided, warring kingdoms—some strong, others weak—that grew out of the mighty Roman Empire."[16] He also gave an overall analysis of the interpretation given by Daniel to the king.[17]

The *New International Version Bible* (*NIV*) recognizes the four major kingdoms mentioned above and then makes this interesting observation: "The diminishing value of the metals from gold to silver to bronze to iron recognizes the decreasing power and grandeur (v. 39) of the rulers of the successive empires, from the absolute despotism of Nebuchadnezzar to the democratic system of checks and balances that characterize the Roman senates and assemblies. The metals also symbolize a growing degree of toughness and endurance, with each successive empire lasting longer than the preceding one."[18] The Apostasy is well known and written about in Latter-day Saint literature.[19]

The stone cut out of the mountain without hands (Daniel 2:44-45)

> And in the days of these kings shall the God of heaven set up a kingdom, which shall never be destroyed: and the kingdom shall not be left to other people, but it shall break in pieces and consume all these kingdoms, and it shall stand for ever.
>
> Forasmuch as thou sawest that the stone was cut out of the mountain without hands, and that it brake in pieces the iron, the brass, the clay, the silver, and the gold; the great God hath made known to the king what shall come to pass hereafter: and the dream is certain, and the interpretation thereof sure.

The kingdom set up by the God of heaven, or the stone cut out of the mountain without hands, has been proclaimed as the restored Church and kingdom by the Lord, angels, the Prophet Joseph Smith, and many, many others. The Lord declared in 1831 that the keys for the stone cut out of the mountain without hands were upon the earth: "The keys of the kingdom of God are committed unto man on the earth, and from thence shall the gospel roll forth unto the ends of the earth, as the stone which is cut out of the mountain without hands shall roll forth, until it has filled the whole earth" (D&C 65:2).

The Prophet declared that seers and prophets "saw the stone cut out of the mountain, which filled the whole earth."[20] Regarding his personal mission to fulfill Daniel's interpretation of the king's dream, the Prophet testified:

> In relation to the kingdom of God, the devil always sets up

his kingdom at the very same time in opposition to God. Every man who has a calling to minister to the inhabitants of the world was ordained to that very purpose in the Grand Council of heaven before this world was. I suppose I was ordained to this very office in that Grand Council. It is the testimony that I want that I am God's servant, and this people His people. The ancient prophets declared that in the last days the God of heaven should set up a kingdom which should never be destroyed, nor left to other people; and the very time that was calculated on, this people were struggling to bring it out. He that arms himself with gun, sword, or pistol, except in the defense of truth, will sometime be sorry for it. I never carry any weapon with me bigger than my penknife. When I was dragged before the cannon and muskets in Missouri, I was unarmed. God will always protect me until my mission is fulfilled.

I calculate to be one of the instruments of setting up the kingdom of Daniel by the word of the Lord, and I intend to lay a foundation that will revolutionize the whole world.[21]

President Brigham Young also testified that the Church was the kingdom of God that Daniel saw.

The God of heaven showed Nebuchadnezzar that this kingdom would never be destroyed; and that is my testimony. This is the kingdom of heaven—the kingdom of God which Daniel saw—the kingdom that was revealed to King Nebuchadnezzar and interpreted to him by the Prophet Daniel. This is the kingdom that was to be set up in the last days. It is like a stone taken from the mountain without hands, with all its roughness, with all its disfigured appearance—uncomely—even a stumbling-block and a stone of offense to the nations of the earth. This is the kingdom that is set up; and the history of the kingdoms of this world all understand, or can read and understand it.[22]

In his history, the Prophet identified several scriptures quoted to him by the angel Moroni and then added, "He quoted many other passages of scriptures, and offered many explanations which cannot be mentioned here" (Joseph Smith History 1:41).[23] One of these, according to President Wilford Woodruff, was the second chapter of Daniel: "When the angel of God delivered this message to Joseph Smith he told him the heavens were full of judgments; that the Lord Almighty had set his hand to establish the kingdom that Daniel saw and prophesied about, as recorded in the second chapter of Daniel; and that the Gospel had to be preached to all nations under heaven as a witness to them before the end should come, and that, too, in fulfillment of the revelation of God, as given here in the Old and New Testaments."[24]

President Woodruff also said "in the name of Israel's God" that God proclaimed through Daniel of his latter-day kingdom.

> The God of heaven also proclaimed through Daniel, 4,000 [sic] years ago, that in the latter days he would set up a kingdom which should never be destroyed; and the kingdom should not be left to other people, but it should break in pieces and consume all these kingdoms, and it should stand forever. That prophet also declared that a little stone should be cut out of the mountain without hands; that the stone should become a great mountain and fill the whole earth; and that it should break in pieces all other kingdoms. Was that Prophet inspired by the Spirit and power of God? I say in the name of Israel's God he was, and so was Isaiah when he spoke of the gathering of the people unto the mountains of Israel to establish the Zion of God in its beauty, strength, power and glory.[25]

In the vision shown to President Joseph F. Smith on 3 October 1918, he recorded that he saw "Daniel, who foresaw and foretold the establishment of the kingdom of God in the latter days, never again to be destroyed nor given to other people" (D&C 138:44). President Spencer W. Kimball also quoted Daniel in support of the Church as the kingdom of God: "This is the restored church. This is the kingdom of God upon the earth, for it is Jesus Christ who organized this kingdom." He then interpreted "these kings" (Daniel 2:44) as "the group of European nations" and said further, "This is a revelation concerning the history of the world, when one world power would supersede another until there would be numerous smaller kingdoms to share the control of the earth. And it was in the days of these kings that power would not be given to men, but the God of heaven would set up a kingdom—the kingdom of God upon the earth, which should never be destroyed nor left to other people."[26]

Elder LeGrand Richards reasoned that the kingdom could not be set up without a prophet. "How could God set up such a kingdom as that which would endure forever without a prophet through whom he could work to establish his kingdom? . . . It would be a stone, cut without hands—in other words, it would have a small beginning, and this kingdom started with six men and has grown, as Daniel said it would, to become a great mountain and fill the whole earth. (See Daniel 2:35.) No other group of religious worshipers is growing by leaps and bounds as is this church today, because the God of heaven has established it according to his promise."[27]

After giving probably the best analysis of Daniel chapter two, too lengthy for inclusion here, Elder Orson Pratt identified the mountain from which the stone would be cut out as America. He explained:

> The location of the stone of the mountain could not be in Asia, Africa, or Europe, nor upon any distant island of the sea; but it must be in America, near the extremities of the feet and toes. This mountain kingdom could not be found in the low countries of America, but in some high, elevated region. There is no country which would better answer the terms of the predicted location than that elevated region bordering upon the great Rocky Mountain chain. A kingdom in that high region might well be called a mountain kingdom, and be thus designated by the inspired Daniel. Its proximity to the western extremity of the image would almost preclude the idea of any other mountainous location.[28]

On another occasion he said, "The mountain referred to by Daniel is the place where the standard is to be raised and the ensign is to be reared; the same place whence the proclamation was to go to all the dwellers on the face of the earth requiring them to listen to the same, and to see the stone that was cut out of the mountains that was eventually to fill the whole earth; while the great image representing all human governments was to become like the chaff of the summer threshing floor."[29]

Elder Orson Pratt also foretold how the stone cut out of the mountain would break in pieces the kingdoms:

> When God has fulfilled the saying written by the Prophet Daniel, there will be one universal kingdom, and only one, and that will be kingdom of God, and Jesus himself will be the great king. Inquires one—"What do you mean by this breaking to pieces? Do you think Daniel meant that they should go forth with physical force and subdue all the nations?" No, I do not think any such thing; but when the Lord God sends his holy

angel from heaven with the everlasting Gospel and then ordains his servants to the Apostleship, and sends them forth among the nations of the earth, and they proclaim the Gospel of the kingdom among the people, if the people will not hear, the Lord himself will break them in pieces. It will be the message that he sends that will ripen them for destruction.[30]

The prophet Jeremiah prophesied of "a full end of all nations" (Jeremiah 30:11). The Lord confirmed that "a full end of all nations" would come after the inhabitants of the earth had felt "the wrath, and indignation, and chastening hand of an Almighty God" (D&C 87:6). These prophecies point to the Millennium, and also as the final time period that was seen by Daniel.

As mentioned by Elder Pratt earlier in this chapter, there will be only one kingdom when Daniel's prophecy has fully been fulfilled. President Ezra Taft Benson stated, "The Church of Jesus Christ of Latter-day Saints is, as Daniel prophesied, a spiritual kingdom 'cut out of the mountain without hands' (Daniel 2:45), meaning that it was begun through the intervention of God. It is not just another human institution. What other organizations or churches ascribe their founding to the declaration that messengers have come to human beings from the God of heaven with authority and power to restore ordinances and keys lost by apostasy?"[31]

President John Taylor spoke of the political kingdom of God as well as the Church: "Now as to the great future what shall we say? Why, a little stone has been cut out of the mountains without hands, and this little stone is becoming a great nation, and it will eventually fill the whole earth. How will it fill it, religiously? Yes, and politically too, for it will have the rule, the power, the authority, the dominion in its own hands. This is the position that we are destined to occupy."[32] He also qualified the meaning of the kingdom of heaven.

> It is called the kingdom of God, or the kingdom of heaven. If, therefore, it is the kingdom of heaven, it must receive its laws, organization, and government, from heaven; for if they were earthly, then would they be like those on the earth. The kingdom of heaven must therefore be the government, and laws of heaven, on the earth. If the government and laws of heaven are known and observed on the earth, they must be communicated, or revealed from the heavens to the earth. These things are plain

and evident, if we are to have any kingdom of heaven, for it is very clear, that if it is not God's rule, it cannot be his government, and it is as evident that if it is not revealed from heaven it cannot be the kingdom of heaven.[33]

One common interpretation of Daniel's prophecy of the kingdom being set up is the establishment of the Christian church in the meridian of times. This interpretation is refuted by the scriptures. Daniel told the king that the God in Heaven "maketh known to the king Nebuchadnezzar what shall be in the latter days" (2:28). While there are other interpretations of the latter days, the meridian of times was not the latter days. Daniel also said that the kingdom he saw established "shall never be destroyed" (2:44). A restoration of the gospel was foretold by the Old Testament prophets and the New Testament apostles. Peter spoke of "the times of refreshing shall come from the presence of the Lord; And he shall send Jesus Christ, which before was preached unto you: Whom the heaven must receive until the times of restitution of all things, which God hath spoken by the mouth of all his holy prophets since the world began" (Acts 3:19–21). There need not be a restoration if the kingdom had remained on the earth. Paul warned the Thessalonians "that ye be not soon shaken in mind, or be troubled, neither by spirit, nor by word, nor by letter as from us, as that the day of Christ is at hand. Let no man deceive you by any means: *for that day shall not come,* except there come a falling away first, and that man of sin be revealed, the son of perdition" (2 Thessalonians 2:2–3, italics added; see also Matthew 24:4–5; Acts 20:28–30). The Apostasy does not sustain the interpretation that Daniel's prophecy refers to the Church at the time of Christ.

Daniel also said that "the kingdom shall not be left to another people" (2:44). In a parable to the wicked Pharisees, Jesus said, "Therefore say I unto you, The kingdom of God shall be taken from you, and given to a nation bringing forth the fruits thereof" (Matthew 21:43). The kingdom was taken from the Jews and given to the Gentiles (Acts 13:46–47). The Jews rejected the gospel first. The Twelve were sent first only to the house of Israel (Matthew 10:5–6), and Jesus himself was not sent to the Gentiles (Matthew 15:24; John 10:16; 3 Nephi 15:21–24). The Twelve were sent to the Gentiles after his resurrection (Mark 16:15–16). Jesus also taught that the "first shall be last; and the last shall be first" (Matthew 19:30). He had earlier taught that many would "come from the east and west, and shall sit down with Abraham, and Isaac, and Jacob, in the kingdom of heaven. But the children of the kingdom shall be cast out into outer darkness" (Matthew 8:11–12). The Book of Mormon verifies that he was referring to the Jews receiving the gospel first and then the Gentiles in his day, and in reverse order in the latter days. "And the time cometh that he shall manifest himself unto all nations, both unto the Jews and also unto the Gentiles; and after he has manifested himself unto the Jews and also unto the Gentiles, then he shall manifest himself unto the Gentiles and also unto the Jews, and the last shall be first, and the first shall be last" (1 Nephi 13:42). In the latter-day restoration, the gospel was to first go to the Gentiles and then to the Jews, or the house of Israel (see D&C 29:30; 90:8–9; 107:33–35). The gospel was taken from the Jews and given to another people—the Gentiles—in the meridian of time, but after an apostasy it was brought back to the Lord's people—Israel—who had been scattered among the Gentiles. These people were commissioned once more to take the gospel to all nations, but in the order outlined by the Savior (see D&C 90:8–9). As the above references will confirm,[34] in the last days, there was a Restoration that was to stand forever. It began in 1830 with the restoration of the Church and will continue through the Millennium and into eternity.

Elder Parley P. Pratt said this political kingdom would come when the times of the Gentiles are fulfilled: "Now, when the times of the Gentiles are fulfilled there will be an uprooting of their governments and institutions, and of their civil, political, and religious polity. There will be a shaking of nations, a downfall of empires, an upturning of thrones and dominions, as Daniel has foretold, and the kingdom and power, and rule on the earth will return to another people, and exist under another polity, as Daniel has further foretold."[35]

President Joseph Fielding Smith spoke plainly of the kingdom standing forever in light of apostates:

> The proper interpretation of this wonderful prophecy is that the Lord has set up his Church (or kingdom) for the last time; it is to grow and increase until it shall fill the earth, and, according to the prophetic interpretation of Daniel, this kingdom shall stand forever.
>
> Now, let us speak plainly and clearly in relation to this remarkable vision and Daniel's interpretation.
>
> This great kingdom is verily the Church of Jesus Christ,

which has been established in the earth for the last time. It is not to be destroyed but is to continue to endure and increase until it shall fill the earth in the due time of the Lord.

From time to time there have been apostates withdraw from the Church. There have been attempts to set up opposition organizations but they do not prosper, nor can they.[36]

President Spencer W. Kimball gave a similar warning to the cultists and critics of the Church: "This one scripture [v. 44], which has been accepted by the Church of the Restoration, should be sufficient to satisfy every cultist or critic of the true Church of Jesus Christ, and should make him not only believe and tremble, but cause him to be afraid to kick against the pricks and to fight against the Church of the Lord."[37]

Nebuchadnezzar acknowledges Daniel's God
(Daniel 2:46-49)

Then the king Nebuchadnezzar fell upon his face, and worshipped Daniel, and commanded that they should offer an oblation and sweet odours unto him.

The king answered unto Daniel, and said, Of a truth it is, that your God is a God of gods, and a Lord of kings, and a revealer of secrets, seeing thou couldest reveal this secret.

Then the king made Daniel a great man, and gave him many great gifts, and made him ruler over the whole province of Babylon, and chief of the governors over all the wise men of Babylon.

Then Daniel requested of the king, and he set Shadrach, Meshach, and Abed-nego, over the affairs of the province of Babylon: but Daniel sat in the gate of the king.

The Lord had established Daniel as his servant in the eyes of the great worldly king. Daniel extended his blessing to his friends: Shadrach, Meshach, and Abed-nego. Collectively, they were in a position to help the children of Israel, who were in captivity, to live their religion and receive the blessings thereof.

A second vision is later given to Daniel that is a second witness and further verification to us today.

Four great beasts out of the sea
(Daniel 7:1-7)

In the first year of Belshazzar king of Babylon Daniel had a dream and visions of his head upon his bed: then he wrote the dream, and told the sum of the matters.

Daniel spake and said, I saw in my vision by night, and, behold, the four winds of the heaven strove upon the great sea. And four great beasts came up from the sea, diverse one from another.

The first was like a lion, and had eagle's wings: I beheld till the wings thereof were plucked, and it was lifted up from the earth, and made stand upon the feet as a man, and a man's heart was given to it.

And behold another beast, a second, like to a bear, and it raised up itself on one side, and it had three ribs in the mouth of it between the teeth of it: and they said thus unto it, Arise, devour much flesh.

After this I beheld, and lo another, like a leopard, which had upon the back of it four wings of a fowl; the beast had also four heads; and dominion was given to it.

After this I saw in the night visions, and behold a fourth beast, dreadful and terrible, and strong exceedingly; and it had great iron teeth: it devoured and brake in pieces, and stamped the residue with the feet of it: and it was diverse from all the beasts that were before it; and it had ten horns.

Belshazzar is either a son or grandson of Nebuchadnezzar. His traditional dating is about 555 B.C. The date of Daniel's dream is therefore about fifty years after he interpreted King Nebuchadnezzar's dream (about 605 B.C.).

The Prophet Joseph Smith said that the beasts which Daniel saw were kingdoms of the world.

> When God made use of the figure of a beast in visions to the prophets He did it to represent those kingdoms which had degenerated and become corrupt, savage and beast-like in their dispositions, even the degenerate kingdoms of the wicked world; but He never made use of the figure of a beast nor any of the brute kind to represent His kingdom.
>
> Daniel says (ch. 7, v. 16) when he saw the vision of the four beasts, "I came near unto one of them that stood by, and asked

him the truth of all this," the angel interpreted the vision to Daniel; but we find, by the interpretation that the figures of beasts had no allusion to the kingdom of God. You there see that the beasts are spoken of to represent the kingdoms of the world, the inhabitants whereof were beastly and abominable characters; they were murderers, corrupt, carnivorous, and brutal in their dispositions. The lion, the bear, the leopard, and the ten-horned beast represented the kingdoms of the world, says Daniel; for I refer to the prophets to qualify my observations which I make, so that the young elders who know so much, may not rise up like a flock of hornets and sting me. I want to keep out of such a wasp-nest. . . .

What John saw and speaks of were things which he saw in heaven; those which Daniel saw were on and pertaining to the earth.

I am now going to take exceptions to the present translation of the Bible in relation to these matters. Our latitude and longitude can be determined in the original Hebrew with far greater accuracy than in the English version. There is a grand distinction between the actual meaning of the prophets and the present translation. The prophets do not declare that they saw a beast or beasts, but that they saw the image or figure of a beast. Daniel did not see an actual bear or a lion, but the images or figures of those beasts. The translation should have been rendered "image" instead of "beast," in every instance where beasts are mentioned by the prophets. But John saw the actual beast in heaven, showing to John that beasts did actually exist there, and not to represent figures of things on the earth. When the prophets speak of seeing beasts in their visions, they mean that they saw the images, they being types to represent certain things. At the same time they received the interpretation as to what those images or types were designed to represent.[38]

These seven verses (2–8) are interpreted in verses 15–27 and will be commented on in following sections of this book.

The Ancient of Days
(Daniel 7:9–10)

I beheld till the thrones were cast down, and the Ancient of days did sit, whose garment was white as snow, and the hair of his head like the pure wool: his throne was like the fiery flame,

and his wheels as burning fire. A fiery stream issued and came
forth from before him: thousand thousands ministered unto
him, and ten thousand times ten thousand stood before him:
the judgment was set, and the books were opened.

The Prophet spoke repeatedly of the Ancient of Days. When
his father, Joseph Smith Sr., was called as Patriarch of the Church
(December 1833), the Prophet spoke of Adam blessing his posterity in
the valley of Adam-ondi-Ahman and then said, "So shall it be with my
father: he shall be called a prince over his posterity, holding the keys
of the patriarchal Priesthood over the kingdom of God on earth, even
the Church of the Latter-day Saints, and he shall sit in the general
assembly of Patriarchs, even in council with the Ancient of Days when
he shall sit and all the Patriarchs with him and shall enjoy his right and
authority under the direction of the Ancient of Days."[39] Doctrine and
Covenants section 116 was given several years later (1838), identifying
Adam-ondi-Ahman: "Spring Hill is named by the Lord Adam-ondi-
Ahman, because, said he, it is the place where Adam shall come to visit
his people, or the Ancient of Days shall sit, as spoken of by Daniel the
prophet" (D&C 116; see also *Teachings*, 122). A year later (1839), the
Prophet spoke of Adam as the Ancient of Days in Daniel 7.

> Daniel in his seventh chapter speaks of the Ancient of
> Days; he means the oldest man, our Father Adam, Michael, he
> will call his children together and hold a council with them to
> prepare them for the coming of the Son of Man. He [Adam] is
> the father of the human family, and presides over the spirits of
> all men, and all that have had the keys must stand before him in
> this grand council. This may take place before some of us leave
> this stage of action. The Son of Man stands before him, and
> there is given him glory and dominion. Adam delivers up his
> stewardship to Christ, that which was delivered to him as hold-
> ing the keys of the universe, but retains his standing as head of
> the human family. [40]

At a conference in October 1840, Joseph Smith spoke on the priesthood through which God reveals himself to people on earth.

> Commencing with Adam, who was the first man, who is
> spoken of in Daniel as being the "Ancient of Days," or in other
> words, the first and oldest of all, the great, grand progenitor of

whom it is said in another place he is Michael, because he was the first and father of all, not only by progeny, but the first to hold the spiritual blessings, to whom was made known the plan of ordinances for the salvation of his posterity unto the end, and to whom Christ was first revealed, and through whom Christ has been revealed from heaven, and will continue to be revealed from henceforth. Adam holds the keys of the dispensation of the fulness of times; i.e., the dispensation of all the times have been and will be revealed through him from the beginning to Christ, and from Christ to the end of the dispensations that are to be revealed [quotes Ephesians 1:9–10].[41]

The Prophet further described Daniel's vision in these words:

The earth is groaning under corruption, oppression, tyranny and bloodshed; and God is coming out of His hiding place, as He said He would do, to vex the nations of the earth. Daniel, in his vision, saw convulsion upon convulsion; he "beheld till the thrones were cast down, and the Ancient of Days did sit;" and one was brought before him like unto the Son of Man; and all nations, kindred, tongues, and peoples, did serve and obey Him. It is for us to be righteous, that we may be wise and understand; for none of the wicked shall understand; but the wise shall understand, and they that turn many to righteousness shall shine as the stars for ever and ever.[42]

The "thousand thousand" (one million) in Daniel 7:10 are those who held priesthood authority in all dispensations, and the ten thousand times ten thousand (one hundred million) before whom the books were opened are the faithful Saints of all dispensations, according to Elder McConkie:

Who are the "thousand thousands" who "ministered unto him"? Are not these the millions who have held keys and powers and authorities in all dispensations? Are they not the ones who are called to report their stewardships and to give an accounting of how and in what manner they have exercised the keys of the kingdom in their days? Will not every steward be called upon to tell what he has done with the talents with which he was endowed? Truly, it shall be so; and those who minister unto the Ancient of Days are indeed the ministers of Christ reporting their labors to their immediate superiors, even back to Adam, who holds the keys of salvation over all the earth for all ages.

And who are the "ten thousand times ten thousand" who stand before him? Are not these the one hundred million and more who have been faithful and true in the days of their mortal probations? Are they not the same "ten thousand times ten thousand" who are "kings and priests," and who will live and reign with Christ a thousand years? Are they not the ones who shall sing in that great day the song of the redeemed, saying, "Worthy is the Lamb that was slain to receive power, and riches, and wisdom, and strength, and honour, and glory, and blessing."[43]

Four kings arise out of the earth
(Daniel 7:12, 15-17)

As concerning the rest of the beasts, they had their dominion taken away: yet their lives were prolonged for a season and time. . . . I Daniel was grieved in my spirit in the midst of my body, and the visions of my head troubled me. I came near unto one of them that stood by, and asked him the truth of all this. So he told me, and made me know the interpretation of the things. These great beasts, which are four, are four kings, which shall arise out of the earth.

It is probable that Gabriel, who is Noah,[44] is the man interpreting the vision for Daniel, since he was the interpreter in the next vision shown to Daniel (see 8:15–16). The Prophet Joseph Smith said concerning the interpretation of visions: "I make this broad declaration, that whenever God gives a vision of an image, or beast, or figure of any kind, He always holds Himself responsible to give a revelation or interpretation of the meaning thereof, otherwise we are not responsible or accountable for our belief in it. Don't be afraid of being damned for not knowing the meaning of a vision or figure, if God has not given a revelation or interpretation of the subject."[45]

There are many things left without interpretation. Where other prophets have spoken, their comments will be given, or where other scriptures suggest an interpretation, references will be cited, but speculations will not be made on the unrevealed.

Daniel's interpreter in chapter 7 says the four beasts are four kings that shall arise out of the earth. Elder Orson Pratt said, "the four beasts described in the first part of the 7th chapter, are the four kingdoms represented by the great metallic image of gold, silver, brass, etc."[46] In other words, chapter 7 is another account of what was shown to king Nebuchadnezzar and interpreted by Daniel in chapter 2.

A little horn comes up
(Daniel 7:8, 11, 21, 23-26)

I considered the horns, and, behold, there came up among them another little horn, before whom there were three of the first horns plucked up by the roots: and, behold, in this horn were eyes like the eyes of man, and a mouth speaking great things. . . .

I beheld then because of the voice of the great words which the horn spake: I beheld even till the beast was slain, and his body destroyed, and given to the burning flame. . . . I beheld, and the same horn made war with the saints, and prevailed against them. . . .

Thus he said, The fourth beast shall be the fourth kingdom upon earth, which shall be diverse from all kingdoms, and shall devour the whole earth, and shall tread it down, and break it in pieces.

And the ten horns out of this kingdom are ten kings that shall arise: and another shall rise after them; and he shall be diverse from the first, and he shall subdue three kings.

And he shall speak great words against the most High, and shall wear out the saints of the most High, and think to change times and laws: and they shall be given into his hand until a time and times and the dividing of time. But the judgment shall sit, and they shall take away his dominion, to consume and to destroy it unto the end.

The Prophet Joseph said, "The 'Horn' made war with the Saints and overcame them, until the Ancient of Days came; judgment was given to the Saints of the Most High from the Ancient of Days; the time came that the Saints possessed the Kingdom. This not only makes us ministers here, but in eternity."[47] Thus, Daniel is shown that the work of the kingdom takes place on both sides of the veil. President Joseph F. Smith was also shown that "the faithful elders of this dispensation, when they depart from mortal life, continue their labors . . . in the great world of the spirits of the dead" (D&C 138:57).

114

President Joseph Fielding Smith observed, "Daniel and John each saw the opposition the little horn made against the Church of Jesus Christ of Latter-day Saints. This opposition will continue until the grand council is held at Adam-ondi-Ahman. This 'little horn' (Daniel 7:20–22; Revelation 13) is making a renewed and determined effort today to destroy the Church. The Lord has decreed otherwise and while its power will last until Michael comes and the Son of Man receives his rightful place, this great power will endure. It must, however, fall, and according to the scriptures its end will come rather suddenly."[48] The references used by President Smith suggest the great and abominable church (see 1 Nephi 13:1–9; D&C 29:21) is the little horn of verse 8 and that the beast that was slain is the fall of the great and abominable church.

The Son of Man comes to the Ancient of Days
(Daniel 7:13–14, 18–22, 27)

I saw in the night visions, and, behold, one like the Son of man came with the clouds of heaven, and came to the Ancient of days, and they brought him near before him.

And there was given him dominion, and glory, and a kingdom, that all people, nations, and languages, should serve him: his dominion is an everlasting dominion, which shall not pass away, and his kingdom that which shall not be destroyed. . . .

But the saints of the most High shall take the kingdom, and possess the kingdom for ever, even for ever and ever. Then I would know the truth of the fourth beast, which was diverse from all the others, exceeding dreadful, whose teeth were of iron, and his nails of brass; which devoured, brake in pieces, and stamped the residue with his feet;

And of the ten horns that were in his head, and of the other which came up, and before whom three fell; even of that horn that had eyes, and a mouth that spake very great things, whose look was more stout than his fellows.

I beheld, and the same horn made war with the saints, and prevailed against them; Until the Ancient of days came, and judgment was given to the saints of the most High; and the time came that the saints possessed the kingdom. . . .

And the kingdom and dominion, and the greatness of the kingdom under the whole heaven, shall be given to the people of the saints of the most High, whose kingdom is an everlasting kingdom, and all dominions shall serve and obey him.

President Joseph F. Smith commented on these verses:

> "The kingdom and dominion, and greatness of the king-
> dom under the whole heaven, shall be given to the people of
> the Saints of the Most High, whose kingdom is an everlasting
> kingdom, and all dominions shall serve and obey him. . . ."
> "When will the kingdom be given to the Saints?" The answer
> was, "When the Saints become wise enough not to turn it
> right over into the lap of the enemy the moment they obtain
> possession of it, and not till then." There never was a truer say-
> ing than this. It takes several things to make a kingdom. First,
> there must be a king; second, there must be a people; third,
> there must be territory or a place for the people to dwell. Then
> come the laws and the rules of government of the kingdom.
> Now, the territory or dwelling place is a part of the royalty of
> that kingdom, is it not? Could you have a kingdom without a
> place to put it? No. We must have a place to put the kingdom,
> and it is as necessary to have such a place as it is to have the
> king and the people. Now, which is worst, to sell out our inter-
> est in the king, the people or the territory to the enemy? If you
> betray the king to the enemy, you are a traitor. Yet there are
> some people who betray the king; they do not care much about
> Christ, the King of kings and the Lord of Lords, and they sell
> out their interest in Him, or betray Him with very little com-
> punction of conscience.[49]

The kingdom has grown rapidly since President Smith made this
observation, but is there a tendency for some or even many to turn the
kingdom over to Satan and his helpers? As Church members progress
more towards becoming a Zion society, the New Jerusalem will be established—and then the kingdom of heaven will come.

President Brigham Young said, "When the Saints of the Most High
are established upon the earth, and are prepared to receive the kingdom
of God in its fulness, as foretold by the Prophet Daniel, they will have
power to protect themselves and all the sons and daughters of Adam in
their rights. Then, when a person or community says, 'I do not want to
believe your religion,' they will enjoy liberty to believe as they please, as
fully as we shall."[50] The power to protect themselves was shown to Nephi:
the righteousness of the Saints of the Church and the power of God,

or the priesthood (see 1 Nephi 14:14).

Elder LeGrand Richards observed, "Now, it is obvious that a kingdom cannot be delivered unto the Son of Man when he comes to take his rightful place to rule over all nations unless a kingdom is prepared for him. The kingdom, according to Daniel, is to be given to 'the saints of the most High" that they might possess the kingdom for ever, even for ever and ever."[51] The Lord revealed in 1834 that the army of Israel must first become great, along with other requirements, before the city of Zion would be redeemed, and that it must "be sanctified before [him]" (D&C 105:31). Comparing today's membership with that of 1834, the more important challenge remaining for the Church members to prepare the kingdom for Christ's coming is to be sanctified, or arm themselves with righteousness.

Joseph Smith said he "saw Adam in the valley of Adam-ondi-Ahman"[52] and spoke of things that will come before the Ancient of Days comes and "the saints possessed the kingdom" (Daniel 7:22): "It will come as did the cholera, war, fires, and earthquakes; one pestilence after another, until the Ancient of Days comes, then judgment will be given to the Saints."[53]

Elder McConkie made an important supposition regarding Adam-ondi-Ahman that is applicable to all of the seventh chapter: "And we need not suppose that all these things shall happen in one single meeting or at one single hour in time. It is proper to hold numerous meetings at a general conference, some for the instruction of leaders, others for edification of all the saints. In some, business is transacted; others are for worship and spiritual refreshment."[54] The work of the Lord has been underway since the spring of 1820 and will continue until he comes again. The challenge is to personally prepare for that momentous event.

The vision ends and another is given (Daniel 7:28, 8:1)

Hitherto is the end of the matter. As for me Daniel, my cogitations much troubled me, and my countenance changed in me: but I kept the matter in my heart. . . . In the third year of the reign of king Belshazzar a vision appeared unto me, even unto me Daniel, after that which appeared unto me at the first.

"After that which appeared unto me at the first" seems to be saying that it followed the one in chapter 7, or it could be saying it was a follow-up of that vision. In other words, it enlarges upon the first one. Whether Daniel meant the latter or not, the second vision seems to enlarge upon what was shown Daniel concerning the nation of Greece.

The kings of Media and Persia
(Daniel 8:2-4, 20)

And I saw in a vision; and it came to pass, when I saw, that I was at Shushan in the palace, which is in the province of Elam; and I saw in a vision, and I was by the river of Ulai.

Then I lifted up mine eyes, and saw, and, behold, there stood before the river a ram which had two horns: and the two horns were high; but one was higher than the other, and the higher came up last.

I saw the ram pushing westward, and northward, and southward; so that no beasts might stand before him, neither was there any that could deliver out of his hand; but he did according to his will, and became great. . . .

The ram which thou sawest having two horns are the kings of Media and Persia.

The interpretation is given in verse 20: the two horns are the kings of Media and Persia, the breast of silver in Nebuchadnezzar's dream and the second beast shown in Daniel's previous vision.

The king of Greece
(Daniel 8:5-7, 21)

And as I was considering, behold, an he goat came from the west on the face of the whole earth, and touched not the ground: and the goat had a notable horn between his eyes.

And he came to the ram that had two horns, which I had seen standing before the river, and ran unto him in the fury of his power.

And I saw him come close unto the ram, and he was moved with choler against him, and smote the ram, and brake his two horns: and there was no power in the ram to stand before him, but he cast him down to the ground, and stamped upon him: and there was none that could deliver the ram out of his hand. . . .

And the rough goat is the king of Grecia: and the great

horn that is between his eyes is the first king.

The he goat as interpreted in verse 21 is the first king of Greece, or Alexander the Great, who reigned from about 333–23 B.C.

Four kingdoms out of one kingdom
(Daniel 8:8, 22)

Therefore the he goat waxed very great: and when he was strong, the great horn was broken; and for it came up four notable ones toward the four winds of heaven. . . . Now that being broken, whereas four stood up for it, four kingdoms shall stand up out of the nation, but not in his power.

The four kingdoms to stand up (8:22), or the four notable ones, are Alexander's four generals: Ptolemy, who reigned in Egypt; Seleucus, who reigned in Syria; Antiochus, who reigned in Asia Minor; and Antipater, who reigned in Greece. None had the power of Alexander.

One of the four kings destroys the holy people
(Daniel 8:9–10, 23–24)

And out of one of them came forth a little horn, which waxed exceeding great, toward the south, and toward the east, and toward the pleasant land.

And it waxed great, even to the host of heaven; and it cast down some of the host and of the stars to the ground, and stamped upon them. . . .

And in the latter time of their kingdom, when the transgressors are come to the full, a king of fierce countenance, and understanding dark sentences, shall stand up.

And his power shall be mighty, but not by his own power; and he shall destroy wonderfully, and shall prosper, and practise, and shall destroy the mighty and the holy people.

Antiochus IV extended his power from Asia minor over Palestine and subdivided the people of Israel. The prophecy is dual. In the last days, Satan, through his followers, will come against the kingdom of God to destroy it.

The Daily sacrifice taken away
(Daniel 8:11–12, 25)

Yea, he magnified himself even to the prince of the host, and by him the daily sacrifice was taken away, and the place of his sanctuary was cast down.

And an host was given him against the daily sacrifice by reason of transgression, and it cast down the truth to the ground; and it practised, and prospered. . . .

And through his policy also he shall cause craft to prosper in his hand; and he shall magnify himself in his heart, and by peace shall destroy many: he shall also stand up against the Prince of princes; but he shall be broken without hand.

Antiochus IV sacrificed a pig upon the altar of the temple that caused the Maccabees to revolt. Some interpret this verse to be the self-appointment of Antiochus IV as an equal with God. A further possibility is that through his policy, priestcraft did flourish, and Herod, one of his successors, attempted to kill the Messiah with his edict to kill all the children in Bethlehem. That may even be extended to the crucifixion under Pilate because of priestcraft (see 2 Nephi 10:3–5). Again, this will be repeated in the last days, and the kingdom of the devil will fall.

Then shall the sanctuary be cleansed
(Daniel 8:13–14)

Then I heard one saint speaking, and another saint said unto that certain saint which spake, How long shall be the vision concerning the daily sacrifice, and the transgression of desolation, to give both the sanctuary and the host to be trodden under foot? And he said unto me, Unto two thousand and three hundred days; then shall the sanctuary be cleansed.

The length of time being two thousand three hundred days may represent years and refer to the time when true sacrifices will be offered in righteousness in Jerusalem in the dispensation of the fulness of times. The Maccabean revolt began in 167 b.c. No exact time will be proposed, but note the closeness of the date of the revolt plus the 2300 years to the year marking the new millennium.

Gabriel interprets the vision
(Daniel 8:15-19, 26)

And it came to pass, when I, even I Daniel, had seen the vision, and sought for the meaning, then, behold, there stood before me as the appearance of a man.

And I heard a man's voice between the banks of Ulai, which called, and said, Gabriel, make this man to understand the vision.

So he came near where I stood: and when he came, I was afraid, and fell upon my face: but he said unto me, Understand, O son of man: for at the time of the end shall be the vision.

Now as he was speaking with me, I was in a deep sleep on my face toward the ground: but he touched me, and set me upright.

And he said, Behold, I will make thee know what shall be in the last end of the indignation: for at the time appointed the end shall be. . . .

And the vision of the evening and the morning which was told is true: wherefore shut thou up the vision; for it shall be for many days.

As mentioned previously, Gabriel is Noah[55] and the interpreter for Daniel. The vision either extended to the end of the world, with the destruction of the wicked, or extended to the end of the four rulers following Alexander the Great. In favor of the vision extending to the end of the world, the Prophet said one pestilence after another would follow until the Ancient of Days comes.[56] There is apparently a dual meaning.

None understood the vision
(Daniel 8:27)

And I Daniel fainted, and was sick certain days; afterward I rose up, and did the king's business; and I was astonished at the vision, but none understood it. What Daniel saw made him ill for many days. He alone understood it.

Summary of Chapters 2, 7-8

The Lord told the Prophet Joseph Smith, "Do I not hold the

destinies of all the armies of the nations of the earth?" (D&C 117:6). From a study of the book of Daniel, we must answer: Yes! He has foretold the major ruling nations from Daniel to the time of the Restoration. The Lord has verified by revelation that the stone cut out of the mountain without hands is the restored Church and kingdom of God continuing on into the Millennium. The kingdom of the devil will fall, and Christ will reign King of Kings and Lord of Lords (see Revelation 19:16).

Notes

1. See Louis F. Hartman, et. al, *The Anchor Bible* (New York: Doubleday, 1978), introduction to volume 23, for a thorough treatise of the arguments for and against the contents and authorship of the book. See also the appendix to this book concerning the authorship of Daniel.
2. *The NIV Study Bible* (Grand Rapids, Mich.: Zondervan Bible Publishers, 1985), 1298.
3. See appendix.
4. Joseph Smith, *Teachings of the Prophet Joseph Smith*, sel. Joseph Fielding Smith (Salt Lake City: Deseret Book, 1976), 220.
5. Joseph Smith, *History of The Church of Jesus Christ of Latter-day Saints*, ed. B. H. Roberts, 2d ed. rev., 7 vols. (Salt Lake City: The Church of Jesus Christ of Latter-day Saints, 1932–51), 4:78.
6. *Anchor Bible*, 23:14.
7. Ibid., 23:138.
8. *NIV Study Bible*, 1301 n. 2:4.
9. Smith, *Teachings*, 340–41; see also pages 161, 305.
10. Brigham Young, in *Journal of Discourses*, 26 vols. (London: Latter-day Saints' Book Depot, 1854–86), 5:72–74.
11. Smith, *Teachings*, 12-13.
12. Rudger Clawson, in Conference Reports of The Church of Jesus Christ of Latter-day Saints (Salt Lake City: The Church of Jesus Christ of Latter-day Saints, 1898 to present), April 1930, 33.
13. Elder Orson Pratt gave a lengthy discourse on "The Theocracy of God" in 1859, in which he identified the four major world powers as the Medes, the Persians, the Macedonian Empire (Greece), and the Roman Empire. He said the ten kingdoms would spring out of the broken fragments of the Roman Empire that compose the modern kingdoms of Europe and those governments that have immigrated to North America from Europe.

The discourse is thought-provoking and well worth reading although too lengthy for inclusion here. (See *Journal of Discourses*, 7:210–27.)

14. Spencer W. Kimball, "The Stone Cut without Hands," *Ensign*, May 1976, 8.
15. Orson Pratt, *Masterful Discourses and Writings of Orson Pratt*, comp. N. B. Lundwall (Salt Lake City: Deseret Book, 1953), 182–97.
16. Bruce R. McConkie, *The Millennial Messiah* (Salt Lake City: Deseret Book, 1982), 130.
17. Ibid., 126–32.
18. *NIV Study Bible*, 1302.
19. See "Apostasy of the Early Christian Church" in the Topical Guide of the Latter-day Saint edition of the King James Version of the Bible; see also Bruce R. McConkie, *A New Witness for the Articles of Faith* (Salt Lake City: Deseret Book, 1985), 338–44.
20. Smith, *Teachings*, 13.
21. Ibid., 365–66.
22. Brigham Young, in *Journal of Discourses*, 5:75.
23. We know that Joseph Smith shared a knowledge of other scriptures quoted by Moroni. Oliver Cowdery named many other such passages in the *Messenger and Advocate* in 1835. Orson Pratt credits Moroni for information about the Book of Mormon people coming to the American continent given to the Prophet (see *Journal of Discourses*, 17:280–81).
24. Wilford Woodruff, in *Journal of Discourses*, 24:241.
25. Ibid., 25:7.
26. Kimball, "The Stone Cut without Hands," 7–8.
27. LeGrand Richards, "Prophets and Prophecy," *Ensign*, November 1975, 51.
28. Orson Pratt, in *Journal of Discourses*, 7:220.
29. Ibid., 14:68.
30. Ibid., 18:181.
31. Ezra Taft Benson, "A Marvelous Work and a Wonder," *Ensign*, May 1980, 32.
32. John Taylor, in *Journal of Discourses*, 9:343.
33. John Taylor, *Government of God* (Liverpool, England: S. W. Richards, 1852), 89–90; copy in Special Collections, Harold B. Lee Library, Brigham Young University,
34. For a fuller treatise on "The Second Gathering of the Literal Seed," see Monte S. Nyman, *Doctrines for Exaltation: The 1989 Sperry Symposium*

on the Doctrine and Covenants (Salt Lake City: Deseret Book, 1989), 186–200.

35. Parley P. Pratt, in *Journal of Discourses*, 3:135.
36. Joseph Fielding Smith, "What Is the Status of the Fundamentalists," *Improvement Era*, February 1967, 4.
37. Spencer W. Kimball, *That You May Not Be Deceived*, Brigham Young University Speeches of the Year, 11 November 1959, 5.
38. Smith, *Teachings*, 289–91.
39. Ibid., 39.
40. Ibid., 157.
41. Ibid., 167–68.
42. Ibid., 253.
43. McConkie, *The Millennial Messiah*, 584–85.
44. Smith, *Teachings*, 157.
45. Ibid., 291.
46. Orson Pratt, in *Journal of Discourses*, 18:338.
47. Smith, *Teachings*, 159.
48. Joseph Fielding Smith, *Church History and Modern Revelation, Melchizedek Priesthood Manual* (Salt Lake City: The Church of Jesus Christ of Latter-day Saints, 1953), 2:225.
49. Joseph F. Smith, in *Journal of Discourses*, 23:286.
50. Brigham Young, in *Journal of Discourses*, 6:343.
51. LeGrand Richards, *A Marvelous Work and a Wonder* (Salt Lake City: Deseret Book, 1976), 133–34.
52. Smith, *Teachings*, 158.
53. Ibid., 161.
54. McConkie, *The Millennial Messiah*, 585.
55. Smith, *Teachings*, 15.
56. Ibid., 161.

Chapter 7

The End of Times

Daniel 9-12

ll of the chapters of Daniel under consideration in this book were revealed when Daniel served under Darius and Cryrus in the latter part of his life. The exact dates of the several revelations recorded in these chapters are not given.

Much of these chapters fall under what the Prophet Joseph Smith said about not being responsible for a vision for which God has not given a revelation or an interpretation.[1] However, there are many things which can be understood. An outline of the four chapters follows.

1. Daniel 9. Daniel understands Jeremiah's prophecy concerning seventy years of Judah's captivity. He prays to the Lord, and Gabriel comes to give him skill and understanding.

   a. Daniel prays for his people and acknowledges their sins since the time the Lord brought them out of Egypt (9:3–15).

   b. Daniel asks the Lord to turn away anger from Jerusalem and forgive them (9:16–19).

   c. Gabriel appears while Daniel is praying, giving him understanding because he is loved (9:20–23).

d. Seventy weeks are determined upon the people for judgment (9:24).

e. After the commandment to restore Jerusalem is given, the streets and the wall shall be built again after seven weeks and threescore and two weeks [sixty-nine weeks] (9:25).

f. After three score and two weeks (62 weeks), the Messiah shall be cut off, but not for Himself; the city and the sanctuary will be destroyed (9:26).

g. The covenant will be confirmed with many for one week, and in the midst of the week shall desolation come (9:27).

2. Daniel 10. Daniel fasts for three weeks and sees a vision of an angelic being whose words are strong. He is weakened by the experience but is strengthened by another angel.

a. Other men are present but he only sees the vision. The others flee (10:4–9).

b. The angelic being says he was delayed by the prince of Persia for twenty-one days, but Michael came and helped him (10:10–14).

c. One angelic being touches Daniel's lips, and he is strengthened (10:16–19).

d. The angelic being will teach him and then return to fight the prince of Persia; then the prince of Greece will come (10:20).

e. The angel will tell Daniel scripture of truth which only he and Michael know (10:21).

3. Daniel 11. The vision: three kings of Persia will stand up, and a fourth richer king will stir all up against Greece; a mighty king will stand up with great dominion, but his kingdom will be broken and divided to the four winds and not to his posterity.

a. The king of the south will be strong, and one of his princes stronger, and will have a great dominion (11:5).

b. The king's daughter of the south shall come to the king of the north to make an agreement, but she shall be given up (11:6).

c. Out of a branch of her roots, one shall come with an army and prevail against the king of the north and carry captives to Egypt (11:7–9).

d. A son of the king of the south will fight with

the king of the north, but the north will prevail (11:10–13).

e. Many will come against the king of the south, including robbers. The king of the north will come and conquer. He will "stand in the glorious land" and consume it. The daughter of women will be given him, but she will not stand by his side. He will turn his face unto the isles and take many, but his own prince will cause his reproach to turn upon him. He will turn to his own land but stumble and fall (11:14–19).

f. A raiser of taxes will stand up in his estate but be destroyed (11:20).

g. A vile person will obtain the kingdom by flatteries, break the prince of the covenant, and become strong; he will come against the king of the south. The army of the north will be destroyed internally, and both kings will do mischief. The king of the north shall return to his own land and be against the holy covenant. He will come against the south again but not in strength (11:21–29).

h. The king of the north will return and have indignation against the holy covenant and have intelligence with those who forsake the covenant. The sanctuary will be polluted and the daily sacrifice taken away, and "they [will] place the abomination that maketh desolate." Those who do wickedly against the covenant shall be corrupt, but those who know God shall be strong. Many who understand will fall by the sword and by captivity as a purge to make them white at the end (11:30–35).

i. The king of the north will exalt himself, speak against the God of gods, follow the stronger god, and "divide the land for gain" (11:36–39).

j. The king of the south will come against the king of the north but will not succeed. The north will overcome many countries and the glorious land. Edom, Moab, and Ammon will escape, but not Egypt (11:40–43).

k. Tidings out of the east and the north will trouble the king of the north, but he will seek to destroy

many. "He shall plant the tabernacles of his palace between the seas in the glorious holy mountain; yet he shall come to his end" (11:44–45).

4. Daniel 12:1–4. Michael will stand up in a time of great
trouble. Daniel's people will be delivered, many will be resurrected, and the wise will "shine as the brightness of the firmament." Daniel seals the book until the time of the end.
Knowledge will increase.

5. Daniel 12:5–13. Daniel sees two men and asks when the end
of these things will be. He is told it will be "for a time, times,
and a half," but Daniel does not understand.

   a. Daniel is told that the words are sealed up. Many
   will be purified and tried, but the wicked will not
   understand and the wise will (12:9–10).

   b. There will be a thousand two hundred and ninety
   days from the time the daily sacrifice is taken
   away (12:11).

   c. Blessed is he who comes to the thousand three
   hundred and five and thirty days (12:12).

   d. Daniel will stand in his lot at the end of the days
   (12:13).

Notes and Commentary

Very few of the general authorities have commented on these
verses, but some have and are included here. The Prophet Joseph Smith
made one correction in his translation and made a few other relevant
comments. While much can be understood, there is much more yet to
be revealed.

Daniel understands Jeremiah
(Daniel 9:1–2)

In the first year of Darius the son of Ahasuerus, of the seed
of the Medes, which was made king over the realm of the Chaldeans; in the first year of his reign I Daniel understood by books
the number of the years, whereof the word of the Lord came to
Jeremiah the prophet, that he would accomplish seventy years in
the desolations of Jerusalem.

The merger of the Medes and Persians came in 538 B.C. (traditional
dating) under Cyrus the Persian. Although there was more than one

Darius, this was apparently the first Darius. He was probably a sub-ruler under Cyrus at this time.

Daniel's understanding of Jeremiah's prophecy that Judah "shall serve the king of Babylon seventy years" (Jeremiah 25:11) is often not understood. Jerusalem was not destroyed until 586 B.C. (traditional dating). Seventy years later would be 516 B.C. However, the seventy-year captivity began in the third year of Jehoiakim (2 Kings 24:1–2, 606 B.C., traditional dating; see also Daniel 1:1). Seventy years from 606 B.C. would be about 537 B.C. The traditional date of Cyrus' decree allowing the Jews to return to Jerusalem (Ezra 1:1–4) is also about 537 B.C. It does not say what books Daniel was studying, but Daniel was taken into Babylon the year the captivity began (Daniel 1:1). Apparently Daniel had determined that the prophecy of Jeremiah should soon be fulfilled.

Daniel asks the Lord to forgive Jerusalem
(Daniel 9:3–19)

And I set my face unto the Lord God, to seek by prayer and supplications, with fasting, and sackcloth, and ashes: And I prayed unto the Lord my God, and made my confession, and said, O Lord, the great and dreadful God, keeping the covenant and mercy to them that love him, and to them that keep his commandments;

We have sinned, and have committed iniquity, and have done wickedly, and have rebelled, even by departing from thy precepts and from thy judgments:

Neither have we hearkened unto thy servants the prophets, which spake in thy name to our kings, our princes, and our fathers, and to all the people of the land.

O Lord, righteousness belongeth unto thee, but unto us confusion of faces, as at this day; to the men of Judah, and to the inhabitants of Jerusalem, and unto all Israel, that are near, and that are far off, through all the countries whither thou hast driven them, because of their trespass that they have trespassed against thee.

O Lord, to us belongeth confusion of face, to our kings, to our princes, and to our fathers, because we have sinned against thee. To the Lord our God belong mercies and forgivenesses, though we have rebelled against him;

Neither have we obeyed the voice of the Lord our God,

to walk in his laws, which he set before us by his servants the prophets.

Yea, all Israel have transgressed thy law, even by departing, that they might not obey thy voice; therefore the curse is poured upon us, and the oath that is written in the law of Moses the servant of God, because we have sinned against him.

And he hath confirmed his words, which he spake against us, and against our judges that judged us, by bringing upon us a great evil: for under the whole heaven hath not been done as hath been done upon Jerusalem.

As it is written in the law of Moses, all this evil is come upon us: yet made we not our prayer before the Lord our God, that we might turn from our iniquities, and understand thy truth.

Therefore hath the Lord watched upon the evil, and brought it upon us: for the Lord our God is righteous in all his works which he doeth: for we obeyed not his voice.

And now, O Lord our God, that hast brought thy people forth out of the land of Egypt with a mighty hand, and hast gotten thee renown, as at this day; we have sinned, we have done wickedly.

O Lord, according to all thy righteousness, I beseech thee, let thine anger and thy fury be turned away from thy city Jerusalem, thy holy mountain: because for our sins, and for the iniquities of our fathers, Jerusalem and thy people are become a reproach to all that are about us.

Now therefore, O our God, hear the prayer of thy servant, and his supplications, and cause thy face to shine upon thy sanctuary that is desolate, for the Lord's sake.

O my God, incline thine ear, and hear; open thine eyes, and behold our desolations, and the city which is called by thy name: for we do not present our supplications before thee for our righteousnesses, but for thy great mercies.

O Lord, hear; O Lord, forgive; O Lord, hearken and do; defer not, for thine own sake, O my God: for thy city and thy people are called by thy name.

These verses, as outlined in the beginning of this chapter, are self-explanatory. Daniel is greatly concerned for his people and prays for them. He acknowledges their sins and asks the Lord to turn his anger and forgive them.

Gabriel comes again to Daniel
(Daniel 9:20-23)

And whiles I was speaking, and praying, and confessing my sin and the sin of my people Israel, and presenting my supplication before the Lord my God for the holy mountain of my God;

Yea, whiles I was speaking in prayer, even the man Gabriel, whom I had seen in the vision at the beginning, being caused to fly swiftly, touched me about the time of the evening oblation.

And he informed me, and talked with me, and said, O Daniel, I am now come forth to give thee skill and understanding. At the beginning of thy supplications the commandment came forth, and I am come to shew thee; for thou art greatly beloved: therefore understand the matter, and consider the vision.

Gabriel comes again to Daniel. Elder Bruce R. McConkie explains why Gabriel is sent as a messenger. Elder McConkie's message directly refers to a later appearance, but the same answer applies here.

Adam, who is Michael, holds the keys of the priesthood "from generation to generation," and "Noah, who is Gabriel . . . stands next in authority to Adam in the Priesthood." What could be more fitting, then, than for Michael, who presides over the angels and directs their labors, to send Gabriel, his next in command, to announce to the mortals involved those things they needed to know concerning the Promised Messiah and his Elias?

It may even be that, as Michael is in charge of all things (under Christ), so Gabriel is in charge (under Michael) of those angelic ministrations which speak of Messiah's coming, and that either he or those serving under him make the necessary visitations to mortals. In this connection it was "the man Gabriel" himself who came to Daniel to tell that worthy one of the coming of "Messiah the Prince" who would "make reconciliation for iniquity" and "bring in everlasting righteousness." (Daniel 9:20-27)[2]

Daniel's worthiness (verse 23) should also be noted; he was greatly loved. When we love God, we keep his commandments (see John 15:10; 1 John 5:1-3).

Seventy weeks for judgment
(Daniel 9:24)

> Seventy weeks are determined upon thy people and upon
> thy holy city, to finish the transgression, and to make an end
> of sins, and to make reconciliation for iniquity, and to bring in
> everlasting righteousness, and to seal up the vision and proph-
> ecy, and to anoint the most Holy.

Gabriel listed six purposes for the seventy weeks, which is apparently seventy years of the captivity but may also have reference to other
seventy-week periods. The six possible purposes are:

1. To finish the transgressions—to fulfill the seventy-year
   bondage and pay the demands of justice for refusing mercy.
   The captivity came to the Jews because they rejected the
   warnings of the prophets to repent and live the law of Moses,
   which would bring them to Christ (see Galations 3:24). They
   had refused the mercy of Jehovah; therefore, they had to suffer
   the demands of justice (see Alma 42:22).
2. To make an end of sin—to enable those in captivity to overcome the traditions of their fathers, which had taken "away
   light and truth" (D&C 93:39). Once again they had chosen
   to follow the natural enticements of man rather than fulfill
   the law of Moses.
3. To make reconciliation for iniquity—to make restitution
   under the law of repentance, or in the broader sense, for Christ
   to atone for our sins.
4. To bring in everlasting righteousness—to provide an opportunity for the people to be righteous under the higher law. This is
   probably a future purpose to help them become a Zion people.
5. To seal up the vision and prophecy—to show that God does
   fulfill the prophets' words (see D&C 1:18).
6. To anoint the most Holy—to recognize Jehovah as the God
   of the Israelites and acknowledge him as the King of Kings.

It seems plausible that these purposes are dual in nature, particularly in light of Elder McConkie's suggestion that Gabriel is to
announce the Messiah's words. Elder McConkie ties in the third
and fourth purposes with the Messiah's coming: "'The man Gabriel'
came to Daniel and taught him that 'Messiah the Prince' should
come 'to make reconciliation for iniquity, and to bring in everlasting

righteousness' (Daniel 9:24–25). That is to say, the Messiah would come to make possible a reconciliation between God and man."[3]

Jerusalem and the wall to be rebuilt
(Daniel 9:25)

Know therefore and understand, that from the going forth of the commandment to restore and to build Jerusalem unto the Messiah the Prince shall be seven weeks, and threescore and two weeks: the street shall be built again, and the wall, even in troublous times.

The various weeks mentioned in this verse are not interpreted, and many speculations arise. One possibility follows. The temple of Jerusalem was built about 516 B.C. (Ezra 6:15). The wall was built about 445 B.C. (Nehemiah 6:15). Verse 25 does not state when the time period of sixty-nine weeks begins; thus, it is difficult to ascertain their meaning. If the weeks represent a year each, there were about seventy years between the building of the temple and the walls. Perhaps the traditional dates are slightly off, or the wall and the street weren't started immediately after the temple.

The post-season destruction of Jerusalem
(Daniel 9:26-27)

"And after threescore and two weeks shall Messiah be cut off, but not for himself: and the people of the prince that shall come shall destroy the city and the sanctuary; and the end thereof shall be with a flood, and unto the end of the war desolations are determined. And he shall confirm the covenant with many for one week: and in the midst of the week he shall cause the sacrifice and the oblation to cease, and for the overspreading of abominations he shall make it desolate, even until the consummation, and that determined shall be poured upon the desolate.

There were to be threescore and two weeks (sixty-two), after which the Messiah was to be cut off. In 70 A.D., the Romans destroyed the city and the sanctuary (temple). Again, an exact date is missing. The "many (probably Church members) who had the covenant confirmed for one week" do not give much help, either. It was sometime after the destruction of Jerusalem (probably more than sixty-two years) that the Apostasy was complete, or the sacrifice and oblation did cease, but perhaps not in Jerusalem. While general events seem identifiable, the dates are confusing. In the words of Elder McConkie, "Daniel named the very time, but he used imagery and figurative language that can only be understood by the spirit of revelation. He said that 'from the going forth of the commandment to restore and to build Jerusalem unto the Messiah the Prince shall be seven weeks, and threescore and two weeks.' He said that after that period 'shall Messiah be cut off.' Then he described the post-New Testament destruction of Jerusalem by the Roman Legions" (Daniel 9:24–26).[4]

Elder James E. Talmage equated verse 27 with those fleeing from Jerusalem at the Roman conquest: "Daniel the Prophet had foreseen the desolation and the abominations thereof, which comprised the forcible cessation of temple rites, and the desecration of Israel's shrine by pagan conquerors. The realization of Daniel's prophetic vision was to be heralded by the encompassing of Jerusalem by armies."[5] The revised translation of Matthew 24, now in the Pearl of Great Price, partially quoted by Elder Talmage supports this interpretation: "When you, therefore, shall see the abomination of desolation, spoke of by Daniel the prophet, concerning the destruction of Jerusalem, then you shall stand in the holy place; whoso readeth let him understand" (Joseph Smith–Matthew 12; see also vv. 13–20). The Savior was speaking, in this verse, of Jerusalem being destroyed after he was crucified.

The time appointed was long
(Daniel 10:1)

In the third year of Cyrus king of Persia a thing was revealed unto Daniel, whose name was called Belteshazzar; and the thing was true, but the time appointed was long: and he understood the thing, and had understanding of the vision.

The third year of Cyrus was apparently close to the year when an angel had strengthened Darius the Mede (11:1). "The time appointed was long" suggests it was to happen far in the future.

An angel appears to Daniel
(Daniel 10:2–13)

In those days I Daniel was mourning three full weeks. I ate no pleasant bread, neither came flesh nor wine in my mouth, neither did I anoint myself at all, till three whole weeks were fulfilled.

And in the four and twentieth day of the first month, as I was by the side of the great river, which is Hiddekel; Then I lifted up mine eyes, and looked, and behold a certain man clothed in linen, whose loins were girded with fine gold of Uphaz:

His body also was like the beryl, and his face as the appearance of lightning, and his eyes as lamps of fire, and his arms and his feet like in colour to polished brass, and the voice of his words like the voice of a multitude.

And I Daniel alone saw the vision: for the men that were with me saw not the vision; but a great quaking fell upon them, so that they fled to hide themselves. Therefore I was left alone, and saw this great vision, and there remained no strength in me: for my comeliness was turned in me into corruption, and I retained no strength.

Yet heard I the voice of his words: and when I heard the voice of his words, then was I in a deep sleep on my face, and my face toward the ground. And, behold, an hand touched me, which set me upon my knees and upon the palms of my hands.

And he said unto me, O Daniel, a man greatly beloved, understand the words that I speak unto thee, and stand upright: for unto thee am I now sent. And when he had spoken this word unto me, I stood trembling.

Then said he unto me, Fear not, Daniel: for from the first day that thou didst set thine heart to understand, and to chasten thyself before thy God, thy words were heard, and I am come for thy words.

But the prince of the kingdom of Persia withstood me one and twenty days: but, lo, Michael, one of the chief princes, came to help me; and I remained there with the kings of Persia.

Daniel had fasted for three weeks. His answer would have come sooner had Satan not been so strongly resisting the angel in Persia. His prayers were heard, but the messenger was detained from coming (10:12–13). Michael came to assist the angel. The book of Jude records another occasion when Michael contended with the devil (Jude 1:9). The voice of Michael also detected the devil when he appeared to the Prophet Joseph Smith and maybe others as an angel of light on the banks of the Susquehanna (D&C 128:20).

Other men being present but not seeing the vision (10:7) is similar to the experience of Paul's vision on the road to Damascus (Acts 9:3–9; 22:6–10).[6] An angel appeared to Alma and the sons of Mosiah, but only Alma understood the meaning (Mosiah 27:11–12).

Daniel becomes dumb
(Daniel 10:14-15)

Now I am come to make thee understand what shall befall
thy people in the latter days: for yet the vision is for many days.
And when he had spoken such words unto me, I set my face
toward the ground, and I became dumb."

The context of the vision being what would happen to Daniel's
people in the latter days supports the long time suggestion in 10:1
above. What he saw was far in the future. Ezekiel was also struck
dumb (Ezekiel 3:26). He remained so for some time until the Lord
opened his mouth several years later (see Ezekiel 24:27 and 33:22).
Zacharias was also struck dumb when Gabriel appeared to him (Luke
1:11–20). Daniel's muteness was apparently more from astonishment
or from being physically drained.

An angel strengthens Daniel
(Daniel 10:16-19)

And, behold, one like the similitude of the sons of men
touched my lips: then I opened my mouth, and spake, and said
unto him that stood before me, O my lord, by the vision my sor-
rows are turned upon me, and I have retained no strength.

For how can the servant of this my lord talk with this my
lord? for as for me, straightway there remained no strength in
me, neither is there breath left in me. Then there came again and
touched me one like the appearance of a man, and he strengthened me,

And said, O man greatly beloved, fear not: peace be unto
thee, be strong, yea, be strong. And when he had spoken unto
me, I was strengthened, and said, Let my lord speak; for thou
hast strengthened me.

An angelic being also strengthened Isaiah when he was called to
be a prophet (Isaiah 6:5–7). Because this was not Daniel's first experience seeing an angel and because he had been fasting for three weeks,
he was probably strengthened physically as well as a spiritually.

Scripture known only by Michael and Gabriel
(Daniel 10:20-21)

Then said he, Knowest thou wherefore I come unto thee? and now will I return to fight with the prince of Persia: and when I am gone forth, lo, the prince of Grecia shall come. But I will shew thee that which is noted in the scripture of truth: and there is none that holdeth with me in these things, but Michael your prince.

The angel's mission was to teach Daniel and then return to fight Satan, the prince of Persia. The coming of the prince of Greece may have reference to the coming of the third world power, as previously revealed to Daniel. Satan continues his opposition to the gospel in the spirit world.

Gabriel stands next to Michael in authority.[7] Thus the angelic being sent to Daniel seems to be Gabriel again. Neither the vision or its interpretation were ever recorded, but apparently Daniel was shown things that only Michael and Gabriel knew of, except the Lord himself, and were not to be revealed to the people at that time.

Four kings of Persia
(Daniel 11:1-4)

Also I in the first year of Darius the Mede, even I, stood to confirm and to strengthen him. And now will I shew three the truth. Behold, there shall stand up yet three kings in Persia; and the fourth shall be far richer than they all: and by his strength through his riches he shall stir up all against the realm of Grecia.

And a mighty king shall stand up, that shall rule with great dominion, and do according to his will. And when he shall stand up, his kingdom shall be broken, and shall be divided toward the four winds of heaven; and not to his posterity, nor according to his dominion which he ruled: for his kingdom shall be plucked up, even for others beside those.

A careful reading of this verse shows that Gabriel, or the same angel appearing to Daniel, had also strengthened Darius the Mede (11:1). The Lord holds the destiny of all the nations of the earth (D&C 117:6).

Some interpret chapter 11 as a prophecy from the time of Greece; others see it as a prophecy of the latter days (see 10:14) that has not yet been fulfilled. Perhaps it is both, as "all things have their likeness, and all things are created and made to bear record of [Christ]" (Moses 6:63). In other words, we are dealing with dual prophecy. Elder McConkie applied this prophecy to the future. Bible scholars and historians see it as history now fulfilled. In this book, I give both interpretations where applicable. I have referred to the *NIV Bible* because of its reputation of conservative interpretations and historical accuracy. Other Bibles or commentaries also give similar interpretations.

The interpretation of Bible scholars found in the *NIV* follows: The three kings yet to stand up in Persia were Cambyses (533–30 B.C.), Psuedo-Smerdis or Guamata (522), and Darius (522–486). The fourth king was Xerxes I (486–465), who attempted to conquer Greece in 480 (see *NIV*, 1314–15, n. 11:2). The mighty king with great dominion was Alexander the Great (336–23) (*NIV*, 1316, n. 11:3).

The four winds "not to his posterity" were the four generals of Alexander to whom the lands were divided at his death (Daniel 7:6; *NIV*, 1310, n. 7:4–7). Who they represent in the last days has not to my knowledge been interpreted.

North and south make an agreement
(Daniel 11:5–6)

And the king of the south shall be strong, and one of his princes; and he shall be strong above him, and have dominion; his dominion shall be a great dominion. And in the end of years they shall join themselves together; for the king's daughter of the south shall come to the king of the north to make an agreement: but she shall not retain the power of the arm; neither shall he stand, nor his arm; but she shall be given up, and they that brought her, and he that begat her, and he that strengthened her in these times.

The interpretation of Bible scholars found in the NIV Bible follows: "The king of the south was Ptolemy I Soter (323–285 B.C.) of Egypt. One of his princes or commanders was Seleucus I Necator (311–280). The great dominion was originally Babylonia to which he then added extension territories both east and west" (*NIV*, 1316, n. 11:5).

The daughter of the king of the south was Berenice, daughter of

Ptolemy II Philadelphis (285–246 B.C.) of Egypt. The king of the north was Antiochus II Theos (261–246) of Syria. An alliance, agreement, or treaty was cemented by the marriage of Berenice to Antiochus. Laodice, Antiochus' former wife, conspired to have both Antiochus and Berenice put to death. Berenice's father, Ptolemy, died at about the same time (*NIV*, 1316).[8]

Daniel 11:7-9

NIV Bible scholars' interpretation: Berenice's brother, Ptolemy III of Egypt, captured Seleucus II of Syria (see n. 8).

Daniel 11:10–13

NIV Bible scholars' interpretation: Ptolemy IV of Egypt defeated Antiochus (see no. 8).

Daniel 11:14-19

And in those times there shall many stand up against the king of the south: also the robbers of thy people shall exalt themselves to establish the vision; but they shall fall.

So the king of the north shall come, and cast up a mount, and take the most fenced cities: and the arms of the south shall not withstand, neither his chosen people, neither shall there be any strength to withstand.

But he that cometh against him shall do according to his own will, and none shall stand before him: and he shall stand in the glorious land, which by his hand shall be consumed.

He shall also set his face to enter with the strength of his whole kingdom, and upright ones with him; thus shall he do: and he shall give him the daughter of women, corrupting her: but she shall not stand on his side, neither be for him.

After this shall he turn his face unto the isles, and shall take many: but a prince for his own behalf shall cause the reproach offered by him to cease; without his own reproach he shall cause it to turn upon him. Then he shall turn his face toward the fort of his own land: but he shall stumble and fall, and not be found.

The interpretation of *NIV Bible* scholars follows: Ptolemy V had a rebellion in Egypt. Antiochus gave his daughter in marriage to Ptolemy in 194 B.C. Elder McConkie explained:

Daniel, speaking of that which shall come to pass "in the latter days" (Daniel 10:14), says a king of the south and a king of the north shall each have dominion and power over nations and peoples. Who these kings shall be and what nations shall be subject to them, no man knows. It is sufficient for our present purposes to know that the king of the north shall come with his armies and overrun the "chosen people, and none shall stand before him: and he shall stand in the glorious land, which by his hand shall be consumed." The chosen people are the servants of the Lord with whom he has made the covenant of salvation; and the glorious land is Palestine, the Holy Land, the land promised of God to the seed of Abraham, with whom the covenant of salvation was made in days of old.[9]

Daniel 11:20

NIV Bible scholars' interpretation: The raiser of taxes, Seleucus's finance minister Heliodorus engineered Seleucus's death (*NIV* 1317, n. 8).

Daniel 11:21-29

NIV Bible scholars' interpretation: The contemptible (vile) person was Seleucus's younger brother Antiochus IV Epiphanes. The prince of the covenant was either the high priest Onios III or Ptolemy VI Philometor. Against the holy covenant, Antichus plundered the temple in Jerusalem and massacred many Jews (NIV 1317, n. 8).

Daniel 11:30-35

NIV Bible scholars' interpretation: Those who have intelligence with them who forsake the holy covenant are apostate Jews. The abomination that maketh desolation was an altar to the pagan god Zeus Olympius, set up in 168 B.C. by Antiochus Epiphanes. Those who are wise (understand) represent the Jewish resistance movement, Hasidim. "A little help" was the Maccabean revolt 168 B.C. "Time of the end" was the end of Antiochus Epiphanes (*NIV*, 1317, n. 8).

Religious wars
(Daniel 11:28-29)

Then shall he return into his land with great riches; and his heart shall be against the holy covenant; and he shall do exploits, and return to his own land. At the time appointed he shall return, and come toward the south; but it shall not be as the former, or as the latter.

Elder McConkie wrote:

> After this there will be wars and intrigue, with one king
> following another. Then again a king will come from the north.
> . . . It is a holy war; his armies are fighting a people because of
> their religion. . . . Traitors to the cause of truth and righteous-
> ness will give their support to [the king from the north].
>
> When he comes again, it will be the occasion of "the abom-
> ination that maketh desolate," which we have heretofore seen
> means the fall of Jerusalem again in the final great war. We do
> not speculate as to what nations are involved in these wars. It is
> well known that the United States and Great Britain and the
> Anglo-Saxon peoples have traditionally been linked together in
> causes designed to promote freedom and guarantee the rights of
> man. It is also well known that there are other nations, ruled by
> a godless communistic power, that have traditionally fought to
> enslave rather than to free men. It is fruitless to try and name
> nations and set forth the alliances that are to be. Our purpose
> in alluding at all to these recitations of Daniel is to show that
> Armageddon will be a holy war. There will be political over-
> tones, of course. Wars are fought by nations, which are political
> entities. But the underlying causes and the moving power in the
> hearts of men will be their views on religious issues. The grand
> desideratum will be whether they are for Christ and his gospel
> or against him and his cause.[10]

Those who oppose the everlasting covenant
(Daniel 11:32–33)

> And such as do wickedly against the covenant shall he cor-
> rupt by flatteries: but the people that do know their God shall
> be strong, and do exploits. And they that understand among the
> people shall instruct many: yet they shall fall by the sword, and
> by flame, by captivity, and by spoil, many days.

Elder McConkie commented:

> Those who oppose the covenant that is the everlasting gos-
> pel shall be flattered into joining the godless forces. . . . God is
> known by revelation; knowledge of him is found in the hearts
> of the faithful. . . . The gospel will be taught; the mind and will
> of the Lord will be proclaimed; those who oppose the cause

of truth and righteousness will do so with their eyes open. . . .
These events shall go forward over a long period of time; there
will be ample opportunity for all nations to choose the course
they will pursue; the testing purposes of mortality will be fulfilled. . . .

Though they fall in this life, they shall rise in eternal glory
in the next. Even the saints must be tried and tested to the full;
the Lord is determining whether they will abide in his covenant
even unto death, and those who do not so abide are not worthy
of him.[11]

The anti-Christ
(Daniel 11:36–39)

And the king shall do according to his will; and he shall
exalt himself, and magnify himself above every god, and shall
speak marvelous things against the God of gods, and shall prosper till the indignation be accomplished: for that that is determined shall be done.

Neither shall he regard the God of his fathers, nor the
desire of women, nor regard any god: for he shall magnify himself above all.

But in his estate shall he honour the God of forces: and a
god whom his fathers knew not shall he honour with gold, and
silver, and with precious stones, and pleasant things.

Thus shall he do in the most strong holds with a strange
god, whom he shall acknowledge and increase with glory: and
he shall cause them to rule over many, and shall divide the land
for gain.

The *NIV* and Elder McConkie labeled these verses as the anti-
Christ. The *NIV* acknowledges their designation of Antiochus Epiph-
anes as "time of the end" does not fit to the end of the chapter.
Elder McConkie quoted and commented on verses 36–39:

As the polarization between good and evil continues apace
in the last days, we may expect to see more resistance manifest
by them toward God and his laws. . . .

From the perspective of Daniel, in whose day all men
worshiped one kind of a god or another, what would be more
strange than to worship a god composed of spirit nothingness,
or, as atheists do, to worship a philosophy that says there is no

god. Clearly the great issues at Armageddon are God and religion and a way of worship. Satan will have done this work well; by then billions of earth's inhabitants (even more so then than now) will be in open rebellion against the gospel and every principle of truth and virtue found therein.[12]

A worldwide conflict
(Daniel 11:40-45)

And at the time of the end shall the king of the south push at him: and the king of the north shall come against him like a whirlwind, with chariots, and with horsemen, and with many ships; and he shall enter into the countries, and shall overflow and pass over.

He shall enter also into the glorious land, and many countries shall be overthrown: but these shall escape out of his hand, even Edom, and Moab, and the chief of the children of Ammon.

He shall stretch forth his hand also upon the countries; and the land of Egypt shall not escape. But he shall have power over the treasures of gold and of silver, and over all the precious things of Egypt: and the Libyans and the Ethiopians shall be at his steps.

But tidings out of the east and out of the north shall trouble him: therefore he shall go forth with great fury to destroy, and utterly to make away many.

And he shall plant the tabernacles of his palace between the seas in the glorious holy mountain; yet he shall come to his end, and none shall help him.

Elder McConkie's comments concerning verses 40–41 suggest that this battle would be "a worldwide conflict" with "Armageddon and Jerusalem [as] the central sites," and "some nations shall escape"; then he quoted verses 44–45.[13]

Those written in the book shall be saved
(Daniel 12:1-4)

And at that time shall Michael stand up, the great prince which standeth for the children of thy people: and there shall be a time of trouble, such as never was since there was a nation even to that same time: and at that time thy people shall be delivered, every one that shall be found written in the book.

And many of them that sleep in the dust of the earth shall awake, some to everlasting life, and some to shame and everlasting contempt.

And they that be wise shall shine as the brightness of the firmament; and they that turn many to righteousness as the stars for ever and ever.

But thou, O Daniel, shut up the words, and seal the book, even to the time of the end: many shall run to and fro, and knowledge shall be increased.

Daniel's people (those of the house of Israel) shall be delivered if their names are "found written in the book" (v. 1). The "book" probably refers to the "book of life . . . the record which is kept in heaven" (D&C 128:7). A similar revelation was given to the Prophet Joseph Smith concerning the book of remembrance: "And all they who are not found written in the book of remembrance shall find none inheritance in that day, but they shall be cut asunder, and their portion shall be appointed them among unbelievers, where are wailing and gnashing of teeth" (D&C 85:9; see also 85:3–11; 128:6–7). The Resurrection is easily recognized in verse 2.

President Joseph Fielding Smith said concerning this chapter: "So you see this chapter comes right down to the time of the siege of Jerusalem and the coming of Christ, the opening of the graves and the coming forth of the dead."[14]

President Smith also observed that people are running "to and fro" (12:4) today as they never did before in the history of the world.[15] He had earlier commented on the abundant knowledge in all things upon the earth:

The accomplishments of men, through the inspiration the Lord has given them, but which they seldom acknowledge, are too numerous to mention. This is a wonderful age. Everything, it seems, to make men happy, prosperous and comfortable, to lessen their difficulties and responsibilities, has been given unto them; but still they are in the midst of turmoil, dissatisfaction and distress. While knowledge is increased, as Daniel was told, yet it is not the knowledge that saves. Men have rejected the most important knowledge—the saving laws of God.[16]

Elder McConkie called "at that time" in verse 1 "the time of the end" and then said, "The full impact of Armageddon, of the abomination of desolation, of the final great war of the ages—the full impact shall fall upon the ungodly among men, and only those whose names are written in the Book of Life will find a full measure of security and joy."[17]

The Prophet used the words of verse 3 to encourage the saints to be righteous: "It is for us to be righteous, that we may be wise and understand; for none of the wicked shall understand; but the wise shall understand, and they that turn many to righteousness shall shine as the stars for ever and ever."[18]

What will be the end of these things?
(Daniel 12:5–12)

Then I Daniel looked, and, behold, there stood other two, the one on this side of the bank of the river, and the other on that side of the bank of the river.

And one said to the man clothed in linen, which was upon the waters of the river, How long shall it be to the end of these wonders?

And I heard the man clothed in linen, which was upon the waters of the river, when he held up his right hand and his left hand unto heaven, and sware by him that liveth for ever that it shall be for a time, times, and an half; and when he shall have accomplished to scatter the power of the holy people, all these things shall be finished.

And I heard, but I understood not: then said I, O my Lord, what shall be the end of these things? And he said, Go thy way, Daniel: for the words are closed up and sealed till the time of the end.

Many shall be purified, and made white, and tried; but the wicked shall do wickedly: and none of the wicked shall understand; but the wise shall understand.

And from the time that the daily sacrifice shall be taken away, and the abomination that maketh desolate set up, there shall be a thousand two hundred and ninety days. Blessed is he that waiteth, and cometh to the thousand three hundred and five and thirty days.

The "other two" were who stood on the river bank are not identified. We assume one was Gabriel because of his previous appearances.

The various numbers of days and times are generally assumed to be years or periods of years; while there have been many theories advanced, we have no concrete dates to propose. The other verses seem understandable.

Daniel will find rest
(Daniel 12:13)

> But go thou thy way till the end be: for thou shalt rest, and stand in thy lot at the end of the days.

It appears that Daniel's calling and election was made sure, probably before this declaration. The Prophet said concerning having one's calling and election made sure: "The visions of the heavens will be opened unto him, and the Lord will teach him face to face."[19] The Prophet obtained this last Comforter, as did the ancient Saints. Although the Prophet does not name Daniel, Daniel meets the qualifications he gave.[20]

Summary of Chapters 9-12

There is much more to be revealed about the times preceding the Second Coming of Christ. However, the last chapters of Daniel, as interpreted by latter-day Apostles and prophets, have given us a framework or guideline of the events. We must keep our attention on the present-day Apostles and prophets for further direction.

Summary of the Book of Daniel

Latter-day Saints are more familiar with the book of Daniel than they are with Ezekiel, especially the first six chapters that relate famous Bible stories and the interpretation of Nebuchadnezzar's dream by Daniel in chapter 2. Chapter 7 is familiar to some, but chapters 8 through 12 are fairly unknown, as are most of the chapters in Ezekiel.

Once more, this book is an attempt to help others search and understand the prophets, as commanded by the Lord (3 Nephi 23:5).

Notes

1. Joseph Smith, *Teachings of the Prophet Joseph Smith*, sel. Joseph Fielding Smith (Salt Lake City: Deseret Book, 1976), 291.
2. Bruce R. McConkie, *The Mortal Messiah* (Salt Lake City: Deseret Book, 1979), 1:312.

3. Bruce R. McConkie, *The Promised Messiah* (Salt Lake City: Deseret Book, 1978), 259–60.

4. Ibid., 459.

5. James E. Talmage, *Jesus the Christ* (Salt Lake City: Deseret Book, 1951), 57.

6. The Joseph Smith Translation changes Acts 9:7 to be consistent with Acts 22:9; see footnote to Acts 22:9 in the Latter-day Saint edition of the King James Version of the Bible.

7. Smith, *Teachings*, 157.

8. The following explanations will be abbreviated, but those interested in more detail are encouraged to read the *NIV Study Bible* or other Bible commentaries. Where there is no latter-day interpretation, the text will not be given under the headings.

9. Bruce R. McConkie, *The Millennial Messiah* (Salt Lake City: Deseret Book, 1982), 477.

10. Ibid., 477–78.

11. Ibid., 478.

12. Ibid., 479.

13. Ibid.

14. Joseph Fielding Smith, *The Signs of the Times* (Salt Lake City: Deseret Book, 1970), 157.

15. Joseph Fielding Smith, in Conference Reports of The Church of Jesus Christ of Latter-day Saints (Salt Lake City: The Church of Jesus Christ of Latter-day Saints, 1898 to present), April 1966, 13.

16. Joseph Fielding Smith, *The Progress of Man* (Salt Lake City: Deseret Book, 1973), 376.

17. McConkie, *The Millennial Messiah*, 480.

18. Smith, *Teachings*, 253.

19. Ibid., 151.

20. Ibid.

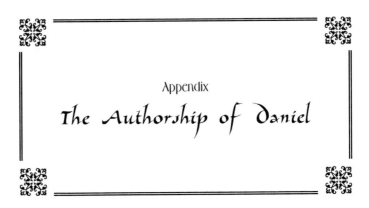

Appendix

The Authorship of Daniel

Many Bible scholars reject Daniel as the author of the book bearing his name. The reasons are many and varied and will not be answered specifically herein. One of the reasons is that it was not included in the Hebrew book of the Prophets but was later placed in the third Hebrew book of scripture, the Hagiographa, or the Writings, as it is more commonly called in English. The date assigned to it is the Maccabean period around 165 B.C., instead of the traditional date 600 B.C.

This work accepts the traditional date because of the support given to Daniel as the author in the scriptures, both ancient and modern, and Joseph Smith's apparent acceptance of Daniel as the author. In Matthew 24:15, Jesus speaks of "the abominations of desolation, spoken of by Daniel the prophet." Would Jesus make reference to a source that was not authentic? I think not. Furthermore, in the Joseph Smith revision of Matthew 24, now incorporated in the Pearl of Great Price, Joseph's revisions included the above quotation concerning the destruction of Jerusalem (Joseph Smith–Matthew 1:12), which was then repeated as again being fulfilled in the latter days before the Second Coming of Jesus Christ (Joseph Smith–Matthew 1:32).

These scriptures are evidence of the validity of the Old Testament text of Daniel's prophecies of abomination (11:31) being written by him (12:4).

In a revelation given to Joseph Smith in 1838, the Lord told him that Adam, or the Ancient of Days, would visit his people at Adam-ondi-Ahman "as spoken of by Daniel the prophet" (D&C 116:1).This revelation supports Daniel as the author of Daniel 7:9-22 and related passages. There are many revelations in the Doctrine and Covenants that speak of Adam and his role at the great latter-day events at Adam-ondi-Ahman (D&C 107:53-57; 117:8).

In a revelation given in October 1831, the Lord uses the wording of Daniel 2:45, "the stone which is cut out of the mountain without hands shall roll forth, until it has filled the whole earth," in speaking of the Kingdom of God (D&C 65:2). Daniel Chapter 2 is thus verified as a latter-day prophecy and indirectly Daniel's authorship is also verified.

Joseph Smith made repeated references to Daniel's prophecies, some by name and some by quoting his words. He identified Adam as Michael and that "Daniel in his seventh chapter speaks of the Ancient of Days; he means the oldest man, our father Adam, Michael" (*Teachings of the Prophet Joseph Smith*, 157-58). Joseph further expounded on Daniel's prophecies of Adam and the keys he holds as the Ancient of Days (*Teachings*, 167-68). In an editorial on "the Government of God" Joseph spoke of Nebuchadnezzar, Darius, Cyrus, and what Daniel saw. He also quoted words from Daniel chapter 7 and 12 without identifying them (*Teachings* 248-54). In a sermon given in 1843, he expounded on Daniel's use of beasts and their interpretations (*Teachings*, 287-94). There are other references to Daniel in the Prophet Joseph's teachings and there is absolutely no indication that he had any reservation about Daniel as the author of the book attributed to him and the validity of his teachings.

There are many prophets and apostles during and after Joseph Smith's day who accepted Daniel and his writings. Many of them are quoted in this work, but there are many others too numerous to mention, let alone quote. Therefore, as stated above, this work accepts Daniel as the author of the book attributed to him.

About the Author

Monte S. Nyman received his bachelor's and master's degrees in physical education from Utah State University and earned his doctorate in education administration from Brigham Young University.

He has served as the director of the Edmonton (Canada) Institute of Religion, director of Book of Mormon Studies in BYU's Religious Studies Center, acting chairman of the Ancient Scripture Department, and associate dean of Religious Education at Brigham Young University. He has taught in twelve BYU study abroad programs in Jerusalem and has conducted many BYU tours to Israel and Central America for BYU travel study.

Brother Nyman retired from BYU in 1996. However, his academic activities have continued since that time. He served as the president of Southern Virginia University from May 2003 to June 2004 after serving as that university's academic vice president. From 1999 to 2000, he served as the university's head baseball coach.

His church service includes a mission to the North Central States and callings as a high councilor, stake mission president, bishop, and member of several stake presidencies. He was chairman of the Church Instructional Development Committee for writing Gospel Doctrine manuals and served for eleven years on the Church Translation and Correlation Committees.

He is the author of four commentaries on Old Testament prophets, as well as two books on the Book of Mormon: *An Ensign to All People* and *The Most Correct Book, The Book of Mormon*. He has also been published in the *Ensign* and *The Improvement Era*.

Brother Nyman and his wife, Mary Ann Sullivan, are the parents of eight children. They have twenty-three grandchildren.